FURNITURE
Making

Plans, Projects & Design

KEVIN LEY

FURNITURE Making

Plans, Projects & Design

KEVIN LEY

This collection first published in 2006 by
Guild of Master Craftsman Publications Ltd
Castle Place, 166 High Street,
Lewes, East Sussex BN7 1XU

ISBN-13: 978-1-86108-448-4
ISBN-10: 1-86108-448-X

Illustrations and plans by Simon Rodway, www.linemine.com
All photographs by the author except those on pages 111, 112 and 113 by Barry Stacey
and used with the kind permission of Lord Barnard, Raby Castle.

Managing Editor: Gerrie Purcell
Production Manager: Hilary MacCallum
Editors: Virginia Brehaut, Gill Parris
Managing Art Editor: Gilda Pacitti
Designer: Jo Patterson

Set in Trade Gothic

Colour origination by Wyndeham Graphics
Printed by Hing Yip Printing Co Ltd

CONTENTS

FOREWORD

Many loyal *Furniture & Cabinet Making* readers will know of Kevin's work and his methods. For those that don't, his great secret is that everything he does is approachable and achievable. He does not use elaborate, expensive equipment or techniques that are baffling. Being self-taught he is not tied to any particular methodology, so is open-minded to new ideas. With many years of making experience under his belt now, this book will give you the benefit of his knowledge without the blood, sweat and tears. Added to this, unusually for a book, the projects are presented with plans included. So there are no excuses, get making, or hide the book so that your partner can't find it – if you want a quiet life.

Colin Eden-Eadon, Editor, *Furniture & Cabinet Making*

NOTE ON MEASUREMENTS

Although care has been taken to ensure that the imperial measurements are true and accurate, they are only conversions from metric; they have been rounded up or down to the nearest ⅛in, or to the nearest convenient equivalent in cases where the metric measurements themselves are only approximate. When following the projects, use either the metric or the imperial measurements; **do not mix units**.

NOTE ON PLANS FOR THE PROJECTS

The following points should be taken into consideration before using the plans in section two of this book.

▸ Components are usually drawn with no allowance for movement of timber.

▸ No rounding of edges are shown for accuracy and clarity.

▸ A minimum of 2mm movement gap all round for solid timber panels is recommended.

▸ **Drawer Frames:** Where possible, allow a movement gap. In the case of mortice and tenon frames, dry tenons can be used at the back of the frame.

▸ **Mortice and Tenon Joints:** Tenons are usually shown full depth in mortices. Allow a gap of ⅛in (2–3mm) between the end of tenons and the end of the mortice.

▸ **Glazed Panels:** Allow for timber shrinkage around the glass – a gap of approx ⅛in (2–3mm) all round.

▸ Doors are usually drawn as an exact fit in their openings with no allowance for hinges and ease of movement.

▸ Sheet components such as panels and drawer bottoms shown are ¼in (6mm) plywood unless stated otherwise.

▸ **Dimensions:** Where multiple subdivisions of an overall dimension occur, such as a chest of drawers, it may be necessary to vary the width or height of a component to fit. Please check all running dimensions against overall sizes before making a project.

INTRODUCTION

The whole process of furniture design and making is magical to me – a great problem-solving binge! Being self-taught, I have never been steered in any particular direction and have always chosen my own design influences, sorting out a method for the making that is within the constraints of my workshop, tools and ability. My method may be slower than formal training – resulting in many mistakes and trips down blind alleys – but it is more fun producing my individual approach. People at the top of our craft, who have very high levels of skill and top of the range facilities, have my greatest respect and admiration for their exquisite pieces. However, I believe that some very acceptable results can be achieved by us lesser mortals – with a dash of skill and knowledge, a basic range of tools, facilities and a lot of application, hard work and organization.

English and American Arts and Crafts and Shaker styles are my main influences. I aim to make straightforward, well-proportioned, clean-lined furniture, with no fussy detail, that does its job well and looks good in the process. Most of the good looks are already in the timber, and my task is to present the timber in the best way possible. As a professional, it is also my responsibility to make sure the client is aware of the range of timbers and combinations available. Our native hardwoods have always been my first love and I have done a lot of work in elm, ash, oak, sycamore and salvaged burr elm. Recently, my range has been extended by a major project in the exotic timber zebrano, which is very dramatic, see page 109. I very rarely use stains, apart from fuming, nothing else looks right to me. A timber with the natural colour to suit the project is out there somewhere.

The making is kept as simple as possible – I never use a secret dovetail when a biscuit will do the job and I am not shy of power tools. There is no credit in doing something slowly by hand if it can be done quicker, and usually better, by a machine. I enjoy the making process, but have no wish to prolong some of the more tedious and repetitive aspects. The traditional Georgian makers would have been in awe of the power tools we have available today and, with access to them, would have made even better furniture. Very few clients would be able to tell the difference between a hand-planed and scraped surface or one that had been properly machine-dimensioned and power-sanded; however, all would be unwilling to pay the true cost difference. We must be careful not to price ourselves out of the market for unnecessary purity of traditional practice, which is often inappropriate given modern materials and products. We also have a responsibility to our clients, ourselves and our craft to do things cost-efficiently. Neither should we undervalue our services. Most makers don't charge as much per true hour worked as they pay to get their windows cleaned. Just because we enjoy doing something it does not mean we should not charge a fair, realistic rate.

Any perceived lack of skill, ability, training, technique, or tools should not be a limitation. Relish the challenge, research and practise and then have a go – you don't know until you try. Strive to find an answer to problems with what is available, rather than wishing for what is not. With the techniques and projects included in this book, I hope to pass on to you the practical answers I have found and save you some of the time and cost of the mistakes, although you will need to invest in the practise.

'It is a wise man who learns from the mistakes of others' – this book is your opportunity to be wise!

Kevin Ley

PRACTICALITIES

UNDERSTANDING BASIC MEASUREMENTS

Measuring Up

Getting your basic measurements right, after consulting with your client, is one of the keys to successful design and making.

Dining chair, bedroom chair and a kitchen chair, all used at tables.

Some feel it is pretentious to describe one's self as a 'furniture designer/maker', rather than 'cabinet maker'. I don't – I put a great deal of thought and effort into making a piece of furniture so that it does its job well and looks good too.

Calling myself a designer is no affectation. What I do is the essence of design at a practical and pragmatic level. There are those who prefer making high-quality work to precise instructions and specifications with no design input of their own. Good luck to them, I hope they make the pieces from my projects and from Simon Rodway's excellent plans and illustrations. However, I like to be fully involved in the whole process, and if I have an idea or contribution I am quite unable to resist sticking my oar in.

SEQUENCE

The first requirement of any piece of furniture is that it will do the job required of it. So that job must be clearly defined and include any restrictions or special conditions that may apply. A bookcase, for instance, will usually have to take specific books, may need to fit in an alcove, blend with existing furniture, or even be stable enough for occasional clambering by children. These factors will affect the shelf spacing, overall dimensions and fixings. All the facts must be known to enable a sensible design to be offered.

THE CLIENT

I see it as my job to ensure the client gets the best I can give and, as a professional, I feel it is my role to offer advice, suggestions and encouragement. The client may have a clear idea of what they want and have difficulty in communicating it, or a vague idea that needs development. I try to put them at their ease by showing them plenty of examples of my work in different woods and finishes.

These may be both actual pieces in my cottage or photographs. I can usually quite quickly get a feel for their likes and dislikes, and slant my contribution accordingly. I try to make the whole process a pleasant experience by being enthusiastic and patient, above all I listen to their wishes and try to avoid imposing mine. I always assume nothing. My clients are my most important assets – I want them to enjoy the experience and take pride in their contribution to the design, which, of course, will become 'theirs'. Then they come back and hopefully bring their friends!

COST

Reassurance about costs is often needed. I advise them that if they are having it made, have it made right. Clients should tell me exactly what they want then, if necessary, we will work out the best compromise for the budget.

Often they are surprised that a small, relatively unimportant detail has large cost implications, and are happy to change the specification. I do not give 'guestimates' but produce a firm price, in writing, together with specifications and scaled, measured line drawings.

These are provided after I have had plenty of time to consider the project in detail. Some clients are prepared to tell me what the budget is and ask me to offer options.

FUNCTIONAL FACTORS

The characteristics of the timber and the finish to be used must suit the piece, its use and the conditions in which it will live. It must be strong enough to bear likely loads and tough enough for intended use.

A child's toy box and a kitchen table will need a tougher finish than a display table. Moisture levels will be higher in a bathroom or kitchen, increasing wood movement, so extra allowances need to be made. I find out as much as I can and consider all the factors relative to the design.

MEASUREMENTS

A main consideration is that the design is within the capability of my facilities and my time. That's not to say that I don't relish a challenge, as I have taken on jobs that stretched me and my workshop to our limits. Given that basic caveat, I keep in mind the following principles and measurements, which have become generally accepted in our craft.

SEATING

A chair can be tailored, with measurements that will be specific to the user. The more usual practice is that chairs are standard and people adjust!

The standard seat height of a side or dining chair used in conjunction with a table, is 17in (430mm) or so, remembering to allow for any reduction caused by upholstery compression. Seats are generally not sloped, the width should be about 15in (380mm) and depth at least the same. In a carver, the seat height is the same but the width should be increased to around 18in (460mm) as the body is contained between the arms and can't 'overflow' the seat.

Rocker – check for centre of gravity, before fitting rockers.

The top of the arms should be about 9in (230mm) above the seat, so that the shoulders are not raised when the elbows are resting on the chair arms. Easy chairs are generally a little lower with a deeper seat, sloped down to the back, which is raked and high enough to rest the head. This allows a relaxed and restful seating position with the feet on the floor, and full support from the back of the knee joint all along the thighs, back and neck, to the head. I generally prefer to make the back rake adjustable. The same rules apply to rocking chairs, but care should be taken when positioning the chair on the rockers. The resting positions of the chair with and without an occupant may be different. The weight and position of the user should be taken into account to see where the centre of gravity lies. Stools have different purposes, so individual measurements apply.

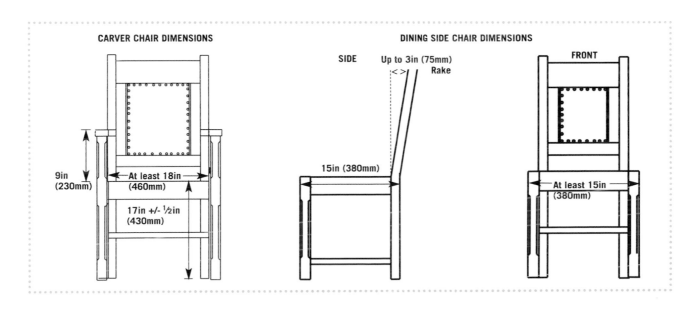

CARVER CHAIR DIMENSIONS

9in (230mm)
At least 18in (460mm)
17in +/- ½in (430mm)

DINING SIDE CHAIR DIMENSIONS

SIDE
Up to 3in (75mm) Rake
15in (380mm)

FRONT
At least 15in (380mm)

Nest of three elm tables with polyurethane finish. It's practically bomb-proof and has been used and abused over 20 years.

TABLES

I generally make tables that are used with chairs between 29in (735mm) and 30in (760mm) high. I allow a place setting 24in (610mm) in width (elbow room) by 15in (380mm) depth per person around the perimeter and, if a chair is between legs, at least 21in (535mm) clearance between them. The width of the top depends on its use – centre space must be allowed for decorations, serving dishes and the like. I would allow 36in (915mm) minimum width for a table with sitters at each side. Extra length must be allowed if the end positions are used so that the place setting areas do not overlap. On circular tables, the place setting must fit into the segment allocated, allowing for the taper towards the centre.

Dining tables in particular may need to seat four for everyday purposes, and eight or more on special occasions, and there are various methods used to achieve this. One of the earliest is the draw leaf table, where the extending leaves are stored under the top and drawn out when required. Variations include drop-in loose-leaf, fold-away-leaf, and hinged-leaf tables. There are also double-top tables, where the leaves fold over on to the top and when unfolded are supported by pivoting the top.

DESKS

Desks follow the general measurements of tables but may need special storage for files or drawings. There may have to be room on the top for a computer and its ancillary kit, plus a light or phone. If the top is much more than about 24in (610mm) wide, drawers and cupboards underneath can become too deep to be practical. In those circumstances, I recommend that cupboards and drawers be fitted at the front and back, thus halving their depth.

Pedestal desks are very convenient as they can be constructed as two individual pedestal units with a drop on top, for ease of movement. As they can be separated, the individual units can usually be moved without being emptied. This was helpful during my many moves in the RAF – all my papers remained properly filed and stored, and were immediately available. Filing drawers can be very heavy and metal runners with bearings may be needed.

Pedestal desk with deep filing drawers. The top drops on to the pedestals for ease of movement. The top is deep, so the pedestal storage is mirrored and also accessed from the other side with a cupboard behind the drawers and drawers behind the cupboard.

WORKTOPS

Working surfaces for standing at, such as kitchen units and counters, should be about 36in (915mm) high, and will be designed for specific tasks.

BEDS

Beds are made to the size of the mattress; slatted beds need an internally sprung mattress; sprung beds should have an old-fashioned kapok un-sprung mattress. Standard sizes are: single: 2ft 6in and 3ft x 6ft 3in (760 and 910 x 1900mm); double: 4ft 6in x 6ft 3in (1370 x 1900mm); queen size: 5ft x 6ft 6in (1525 x 1980mm); king size: 5ft 6in and 6ft wide x 6ft 6in long (1675 and 1830 x 1980mm). Special sizes can be obtained but are expensive.

Beds should break down into component pieces for ease of movement. The top of a bedside table should be at the same height as the top of the mattress.

Slatted bed. Head and foot can be removed to move in three pieces, and slatted platform can be broken down into individual pieces if necessary.

STORAGE

Storage space should be tailored to what is being stored, as far as possible. Shelf spacing, depth and drawer sizes are particularly important.

BOOKCASES

When making bookcases I tailor the shelf heights to the books where possible. Adjustable shelves make for a weaker structure and full bookcases can be very heavy – any attempt to move them might result in cabinet collapse. I make the bases of tall bookcases – and some long case clocks – lower at the back, or chocked up at the front, so that they lean against the wall behind them, for safety and stability.

CABINETS

If possible, I arrange cabinets with cupboards above drawers for ease of access. Shelves are easier to look into without bending and drawer contents can be easily seen from above. On kitchen dressers, I tailor shelves to particular sizes to incorporate cans, bottles, jars, or containers etc. It is surprising how much space can be saved, and convenience increased, by careful analysis of what is to be stored. Several shallow drawers may be preferable to a deep one if a range of small items is to be stored.

Unit for multiple audio units and storage of vinyl records, CD and tape cassettes. There are holes in the back for cable access and venting.

Dresser with tailored shelving and drawers.

Kitchen dresser making use of correct spacing, shallow shelves and racks in doors, to maximize space.

This drinks cabinet was built round a single malt bottle – well, several actually!

A multiple drawer unit with drawers increasing in depth from top to bottom.

WARDROBES

I allow about 54in (1370mm) hanging length for dresses and trousers, more if shoes are stored underneath, and 39in (990mm) for jackets and shirts. The depth required for clothes hung edge-on is at least 22in (560mm). Ties, belts and scarves can be hung on rails on the door insides, which is also a good place for mirrors.

I combine various arrangements of shelves, drawers, racks and long and short hanging space to achieve optimum storage for the particular client. The size of a full-length wardrobe makes access and transport a primary consideration, especially as they usually need to go up at least one set of stairs. In many cases, they must be made in 'knockdown' form, to be carried up in pieces and assembled in the room.

A single wardrobe with short and long hanging space and shelves. Access was good enough for this to be carried in fully assembled.

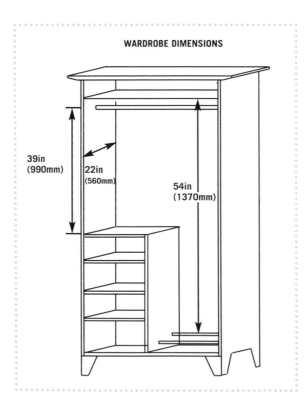

WARDROBE DIMENSIONS

39in (990mm)

22in (560mm)

54in (1370mm)

CHESTS

Blanket chest with trays allowing large items to be stored in base. Smaller items are stored in the trays.

Chests with top access are useful for storage of large items and top trays can be added to increase flexibility. Such a chest with trays made a good sewing box, with material stored in the base, and small items such as needles, in the trays.

A range of drawers can be added under the top-opening chest to make a 'military' chest. These chests were used by military officers in the past and were carried on pack animals. They had reinforcing brass or ironware at the joints and corners and were sometimes referred to as 'mule' chests. Whether this was because they were carried by mules or were a mix of a chest of drawers and a coffer chest is not clear.

CONCLUSION

In summary, one must be able to make the piece, get it out of the workshop, to and into the destination, and ensure it performs its function.

I have tried to cover the fundamental considerations for the function of a piece of furniture. It is really a bit of detective work to make sure you are fully aware of the client's requirements, and then the application of known principles and one's own ability and ingenuity to achieve the aim.

INFLUENCES AND ETHOS

Going to Form

Here I share my design influences and explain the ethos behind my style of furniture making, in which form follows function.

A large, empty farmhouse, which we had refurbished, with no furniture and no money, kick-started my woodworking career in the 1970s. I was at an RAF base where there was a woodwork club with good facilities, and large quantities of reclaimed pine, so copies of the simple and crude pine furniture, popular at the time, started to roll off my production line.

I was initially pleased with my efforts as I was achieving big results from brute force and ignorance. However, I soon became dissatisfied and tried making my functional pieces look prettier. My horizons expanded to include 'proper wood' and influences from classical Georgian and Victorian furniture. Then, in the 1980s, I discovered Thomas Moser and the Shakers, Alan Peters, Arts and Crafts and Ernest Joyce.

THE SHAKERS

The essence of the Shaker belief was honesty and simplicity in all things – 'Beauty rests on utility' – and from this grew their distinctive style of furniture with its superb functionality, clean, unfussy lines and quality of construction. The lightness, delicacy and austere elegance of Shaker furniture have been a big influence on me. Its originators were businessmen, and much of the work was sold to 'The World' i.e. non-Shakers. I do admire their invention of, and pragmatic readiness to use, labour-saving aids such as power tools.

Shaker-style rocker. Contrasting detail, fumed-oak rockers, leg finials, matching seat fabric. Finished in water-based acrylic varnish.

ARTS AND CRAFTS

'Have nothing in your work you do not know to be useful or believe to be beautiful' – the Arts and Crafts initial philosophy of humility and simplicity was in many ways similar to the Shakers, but without the poverty and celibacy.

The designs, however, range from simple country, to ornate 'grand house', and many of the makers had wealthy patrons. Initially, the design influences went back to the Middle Ages, machines tended to be demonized and much was made of handwork. I appreciate the movement's sense of proportion, and the way the visible joints demonstrate the underlying quality of work and the use of native timbers.

Maple Arts and Crafts easy chair arm/leg bracket. Showing $\frac{1}{8}$in (3mm) rounding-over on edges and curve-softening the functional bracket.

Shaker-style side table with elegant tapered legs, overhanging top under chamfered, fumed oak pulls, sealed and waxed.

ERNEST JOYCE

Joyce was a leading cabinet maker in the 1960s, and his book, *The Technique of Furniture Making*, revised by Alan Peters, is an invaluable reference to any serious maker. It contains information on materials, tools, techniques, construction, workshop organization and drawing, as well as examples of the best of modern furniture designs. I have used it gratefully for inspiration and information throughout my furniture making.

OTHER INFLUENCES

Every piece of furniture, drawing or photograph I see has the potential to influence me. Other makers' work in magazines and books, exhibitions, shop windows, museums, catalogues, antiques – anywhere I see it. I am interested in furniture making, and it registers in my brain.

The common features I take from the Shakers and Arts and Crafts makers are individuality, simplicity and quality, which, combined with my own interpretation of the client's taste and wishes, is what I strive to achieve.

DESIGN FEATURES – THE WOOD

Close-up of leg post through tenon in chair arm, showing contrast of end and side grain.

Through-rail tenons proud of leg, with stub ends chamfered and contrasting walnut wedges.

COMPUTER-AIDED DESIGN (CAD)

From the initial brief, I use a computer drawing program to create the design. Most simple drawing programs are more than up to the task. I have been using Autosketch for the last ten years and am still finding new tricks it will perform.

Dimensioned and scaled line drawings of each project are produced and, as usual, I keep it simple – after all, I am a furniture maker, not an artist. The client and I just need a clear idea of what is going to be made and too much artwork can create false expectations. These simple drawings, with a sample of the wood and finish to be used, have always been sufficient, although it is true to say that – unlike some – I have never been asked for a framed copy of the original!

Drawing to scale from the original rough sketches and measurements gets things, literally, into visual proportion. Once the drawing is on the computer it's possible to try different effects, quickly and easily, without redrawing. I find this invaluable for determining the final design.

Both the Shaker and Arts and Crafts makers made much use of a variety of local native timbers, and I welcome that development in modern making. Getting the timber right is a definitive early step. It must have the right physical properties together with the figure and colour to achieve the required look. I try to include design features that enhance its impact and nothing that detracts from it. It sometimes involves mixing woods for contrast of figure or colour.

THE FINISH

The quality of finish and level of gloss is important. I find a matt, natural, almost unfinished look is popular, particularly on light woods. However, sometimes a high gloss is appropriate. The darkening effect of oil finishes can be dramatic on some dark woods. Whatever the finish it must be faultless and staining wood is not usually an option – it never looks right, and I think it spoils the natural colours.

Oiled elm apothecary's chest – burr (burl) elm drawer fronts provide contrasting figure, drawers in 'bricklayer' pattern increasing in depth from top to bottom for visual interest and flexible storage.

TEXTURE

Once people see a piece of furniture, they want to touch it. Open-grained timbers such as oak or ash have a texture to the touch, while walnut, mahogany and sycamore can have a satin smoothness. A light waxing improves the touch factor. Different physical and visual textures can be introduced by using and experimenting with different materials, decorative carving and mouldings.

THE SMELL

The smell of a new piece can be magical – it is usually a combination of wood, polish, blood, sweat and tears. Some waxes contribute to the aroma, and orange or lemon oil on the insides of drawers and cabinets both seal and leave a lingering scent.

I use unsealed cedar of Lebanon components inside clothes storage cabinets and for relevant drawer casings. It has a wonderful and lasting aroma, which also repels insects and moths.

TAPERS AND CURVES

Tapers and curves add refinement. Tapering legs gives lightness and elegance, tapering a carcass towards the top gives a visual stability and balance. Curving rails and stretchers lightens the look. Visual and physical softening can be achieved by the rounding of corners.

EDGE MOULDINGS

I don't use complicated edge mouldings, mainly just a quadrant curve on the top edge, or a nosing by using the same cutter on the top and bottom edges. This rounding over softens the edge, enhancing the feel and adding a highlight. Edge chamfers and stop chamfers have a similar effect.

Ash fielded panel with stop chamfers on inside frame edges.

Stop chamfers on leg post with top edges radiused.

LEGS AND FEET

On tables and chairs, the legs raise the surfaces to a convenient height. Feet and legs on cabinets give stability on uneven floors and make it easier to clean underneath. The more floor visible under a cabinet the less floor space it appears to occupy, hence the current trend to put lights under kitchen units.

In the past, the main function of feet and legs on cabinets was to keep them off damp or even wet floors, which is why so many antiques have new feet. Three legs or feet are more stable than four.

Ash kitchen table and chairs. Crude country design softened by rounding over the edges, curving corners, cutouts and tapering.

Tall lamp table in oiled burr elm, with elegant tapered centre column and three feet for stability.

TOPS AND DRAWERS

An overhanging top can be chamfered underneath to make the edges look thinner and more elegant while leaving the top face flat. The amount of overhang can also be adjusted to suit the piece. For the drawers a contrast of colour between the sides and fronts accentuates the dovetails as a feature. Increasing the depth of the drawers from top to bottom not only increases the storage flexibility but also gives visual interest and stability. I often use contrasting timber on the pulls.

Feature drawer dovetails, casings in sycamore, front fumed oak.

American oak Arts and Crafts tapered china cupboard with overhanging top and decorative brackets. Finished in satin water-based varnish and cut back.

DOORS

I always see a door as a picture with the stiles and rails framing the panel, so I try to make the panel a feature. Deep sawing and book-matching an interesting piece of wood, using a contrasting colour, texture or figure, or a combination of those elements, are ways of achieving this.

Fielding the edges and raising the centre of the panels increases the picture impression. On a pair of doors, it is important that a visual match or balance is achieved. Again, I often make a feature of the pulls or handles.

VISUAL JOINTS

This is very much a feature of Arts and Crafts work, but it can be very labour intensive with cost implications. Rail and post through tenons can be a useful feature to provide visual interest, and pegs of contrasting timber in the tenons increase this. Through dovetails in the same or contrasting timbers can also have a big impact. Visible pegs can be used in mortice and tenon joints. The natural contrast of end and side grain in some timbers is quite marked, and can be used to good effect.

Double through tenons – leg to arm on oak settle.

INLAYS AND CUTOUTS

Decorative inlays and cutouts have their place and I have used them – but not a great deal. They can be very useful to mask a screw head and give the impression of a through tenon, making a feature out of necessity.

Inlays masking screw heads. Oiled fumed oak on oiled sycamore.

BRACKETS AND BRASSWARE

Strengthening brackets can be turned into a feature on suitable work. There is a huge range of decorative brassware available, but much of it is cheap and nasty. Really good stuff is expensive and, I have found in the last ten years, out of fashion. I prefer to make my own handles and pulls out of wood, but something like a military chest will demand the right fittings, although it's worth remembering that originally these would probably have been iron.

Traditional oiled, fumed-oak table with turned legs and brass handles.

CARE AND USE

During discussions, it sometimes becomes apparent that clients do not know how to treat a solid wood piece. They intended it to go in the conservatory in full sun, against a radiator, or some other unsuitable position. I discuss this with them at the time, and now provide a leaflet covering future care and maintenance with every piece.

Suitable conditions for solid wood furniture are on a level floor in a well-aired, normally heated, domestic living area, where it may take two or three weeks to acclimatize to its new surroundings. It should not be placed close to a radiator or fire, in a hot stuffy room, or a cold, damp one. Light may have a gradual effect on the colour of the wood and enhance its patina, but it should not be put in direct sunlight for long periods as this may cause cracking and bleaching. Damp conditions can be improved by raising the temperature, airing the room and, in extreme conditions, using a dehumidifier. Dry conditions can be improved by reversing these, i.e. lowering the temperature, airing the room and, if necessary, fitting humidifiers to the radiators.

CARE OF FINISHES

Wax
Routine dusting with a soft, dry, clean cloth, and a light waxing every six months with a good-quality wax polish following the maker's instructions – and no sprays or silicones!

Oil
Routine dusting with a soft, dry, clean cloth, and a light oiling with proprietary teak oil once a year to makers' instructions. Do not allow a film of oil to build up on the surface – less is best. Allow to cure for at least 24 hours before use.

Varnish and drawers
Tough varnish finishes only require cleaning with a damp cloth and buffing dry. Occasionally rubbing the running surfaces of the drawers with candle wax keeps their action smooth.

CONCLUSION

So much about design is personal choice. There is really no right or wrong, but some things are pleasing to the majority. Influences come from all sorts of places, and it is essential to receive exposure to as many as possible to encourage original thought.

Most clients come to me because they like my work, but their wishes are paramount, and I interpret and achieve what they want and offer, rather than impose, my ideas.

I believe 'less is more', and one or two subtle features enhance a piece, while too many confuse the eye and look contrived. My guiding principle is that of the famous 1930s Bauhaus School of Design: 'Form follows function'.

FINDING A WOOD SUPPLIER

Whither the Wood

Choosing timber can be tricky for the beginner. It is vital to find a supplier of good-quality timber and the following tips will help you source it successfully.

A rack of American oak in a local joinery supplier's yard.

The question I am most frequently asked by clients, other makers, friends and family is not, 'What's yours?' but 'Where do you get your wood?' The answer, of course, is wherever I can, but I do work hard at tracking it down, and I keep a record of who has or is likely to have what I want. Here are some tips for sourcing wood suitable for furniture making.

ASK AROUND

I always ask anyone who might know about local sources of timber. When we moved house I had to ship my wood in from suppliers I knew until I was organized. The local crime prevention officer, while advising on security for the house and workshop, got me started with a few leads. Advertisements in woodworking magazines were another source. I went to an event in the village hall and got talking to my neighbour John, a very helpful local farm worker. He too is a woodworker, and gave me more leads – he also had a nice log of Lebanon cedar in his yard just waiting to be planked.

TELEPHONE AHEAD

Before going to wood suppliers, telephone and explain your requirements, ask if you can select and make an appointment for a suitable time. If, like me, you want to see what you are buying, you will need to select your pieces of timber. This will involve going through stacks and pulling out the boards you want. Make sure that you check if a stack is safe to climb on, and ask for permission and help. Be careful when moving timber and always re-stack any timber you have disturbed.

Timber yards are inherently dangerous places with high stacks of heavy boards and some pretty substantial machinery. Take responsibility for your own safety. Be aware, make sure you can be seen, respect any safety notices, and don't get in the way. Take work gloves, chalk for marking and a measure with you. I also take a small block plane in case I want to check colour, figure, or depth of a stain.

It is worth looking in the Yellow Pages of your telephone directory, and visiting wood suppliers close to you, as a lot of the cost of timber is in the transport. A good supplier will give knowledgeable help, sound advice and have a friendly atmosphere.

JOINERY SUPPLIERS

These can also be a good source of wood. My local joinery suppier is part of a group which has a chain of outlets nationwide. The group imports timber from around the world and holds huge stocks. Its range of high-use, imported timber is very impressive, as are the prices, but they tend not to deal in native UK timbers. As well as hardwoods, they carry a full range of softwoods in various qualities, including the top grade for cabinet making.

An extensive range of sheet materials is also available, with faces veneered in specific timbers as required. There seems to be no problem in selecting the timber one wants, but these are busy places, shifting large quantities to building and joinery contractors, so pick your time and be patient.

Efficient computer stock control will find your timber anywhere in the group if it is not available at your local outlet. A hub-and-spoke overnight delivery system gets it to you at high speed. There is also a decent workshop facility on site at my supplier, and wood can be cut, planed and generally machined. To find your local joinery outlet look in the Yellow Pages and visit to make your own judgment.

A local joinery supplier's machine shop.

Kevin gets a helping hand selecting his wood at his local joinery supplier.

DIY SHEDS

These tend to stock pre-packed softwood and sheet materials with wood-effect surfaces in convenient sizes. They are not cheap, and you get what is there, so buyer beware. They are probably not a source of anything much for the serious maker. However, they do have a very good range of plain and ornamental mouldings, which could be useful.

BUILDERS' MERCHANTS

In the main, builders' merchants will buy their timber from a joinery supplier, and then charge a mark up. This is often convenient for builders, but it is not a source I would recommend. The timber can be poorly stored in conditions unsuitable for furniture or cabinet making materials. If you must buy from this source be very wary.

A good selection of moulding profiles in a DIY shed.

Not the best...timber from a builders' yard – and it's raining!

Softwood from a DIY shed.

A timber supplier's collection of handmade pieces in various hardwoods.

Softwood pieces from the builders' yard.

SELF-SOURCING

When I lived in Yorkshire, I managed to get some good burr elm pieces from my log supplier. I showed him what I wanted, offered twice what he would get for it as logs, and he didn't have to cut and split it down to size. We were both happy, and I got some nice pieces. Some of the bigger ones were cut into small planks on my bandsaw, and others I kept for small projects like cheeseboards, bowls, bun feet and door and drawer pulls. All were air-dried in my wood store, which is dehumidified, and the planked pieces were conditioned in my home-made kiln.

When using wet timber for turning, it speeds up the drying process if it is turned oversize and a proportion of the waste removed. Air-drying takes about a year per inch (2.5cm) thickness, before finishing in the wood store and conditioning cabinet.

One day the log man arrived at my workshop with a Land Rover and trailer on which was a butt of burr, 5ft in diameter and 6ft long (150 x 180cm) – outside the capacity of my bandsaw.

The wood was very exciting, seemed to be sound, it even had spalting in some areas and had come from the middle of a small spinney. It was important to know it was not from a hedgerow, as it might have fencing ironwork embedded in it, a village green, where all sorts might have been nailed to it and grown-in, or an army range – I lived near a garrison – as it might be full of shrapnel!

Some large lumps of burr elm.

The perils of sourcing wood – a huge beech tree with an iron fence right through the middle of it.

DONE DEAL

I contacted a local estate sawmill where they cut fence posts and gates for the estate from their own felled timber. A deal was done and, on condition of an extra payment for each saw tooth lost on a nail and the like, the butt of burr was taken straight there, to be cut into through-and-through boards.

On the first pass, he hit a nail and lost a tooth – should he carry on? I gritted my teeth and nodded. The whole of the rest of the butt was cut into some lovely boards and not another nail was found. That was eight years ago and I'm still using that burr.

PROPER WOOD

Whilst it is important not to miss an opportunity like that, in the main I would not advocate trying to supply much of your own timber. In the far past I was given an oak log and felled a couple of elms on my own land at various times. I had it all planked before I air-dried it and used it, but it was never as satisfactory as 'proper wood' bought from an expert. It just led to lots of wasted time and material.

I am a furniture maker, not a lumberjack, and only in exceptional circumstances – such as for the outstanding piece of burr – would I get involved in wood conversion. It is a skilled job, and one can become a jack-of-all-trades and master of none. Wood is quirky enough when prepared by experts, and removal of as many variables as possible is crucial in our craft.

CONCLUSION

In summary, make sure you never miss an opportunity, always follow up leads and keep records, and take time to register with anyone who might be able to help. Yellow Pages, the internet, personal contacts, tree surgeons, loggers, farmers and local advertisements all have potential. It takes a bit of effort and research but there is plenty of good stuff out there, you just need to find it. And never rely on one source – eggs and baskets and all that!

A burr cheeseboard made from some small, interesting pieces.

RESPECTING YOUR MATERIALS

Stuff and good sense

The making of fine furniture starts with a healthy respect for your materials. The ground rules are few and simple – but ignore them at your peril.

Wood is not inert – it moves – and this must be taken into account when making anything from it. The inherent movement is caused by changes in its moisture content and release of stresses in the fibres during machining. Movement caused by bad making or unsuitable design is a separate issue.

AIR-DRYING

Timber from a freshly felled tree may contain half its weight in water. The first stage in making it suitable for furniture making is to cut it into boards. These are stacked on top of each other, separated by sticks about 1in (25mm) thick to allow free circulation of air, weighted on the top, and left outside to dry.

The stresses released by cutting the fibres of the wood, and those caused by the initial drying process itself, will eventually balance out. This takes about one year per 1in (25mm) of thickness. At the end of this time the wood is seasoned and air-dried to the average humidity level in that place at that time, and suitable for outside use. Very little general shrinkage takes place during air-drying.

KILN DRYING

As there is a considerable difference between outside humidity levels and those inside a centrally heated house, the next stage is to dry the wood to a moisture content suitable for inside use.

The wood, still sticked and stacked, is placed in a sealed cabinet or kiln, and the humidity artificially reduced to the required level. The wood loses more water until it is suitable for internal cabinet work. Most of the shrinkage occurs during this process.

How long the wood has been out of the kiln, and how it was stored before purchase and treated since, can also have a significant effect on moisture content.

Cedar of Lebanon drawer casings sticked, stacked and weighted, to settle in a warm, dry workshop after deep sawing.

Stack of sticked air-drying timber.

SHEET MATERIALS

Stored sheet materials.

Although most of my work is in solid wood I use sheet materials where appropriate. The four main types of board – ply, block, particle and fibre – are all pre-finished, of uniform thickness, with no cleavage line so they do not split easily.

They are stable – for our purposes they do not move when the moisture content changes. The standard sheet size is 8 x 4ft (2440 x 1220mm), and is sometimes awkward to handle. They should be stored flat or upright in dry conditions. It is important that they do not lean or the sheet will bow. Mine are stored upright on the 8ft (2440mm) edge with a turn clamp to hold them against the wall.

PARTICLE BOARD
Particle board (chipboard) is made of chips of wood bonded with resin glue and pressed into sheets. It is heavy, not particularly rigid, and the edges tend to be crumbly. Its main use is flooring, though with lipped edges and a thinly veneered face it is used in cheap kitchen cabinet manufacture.

In one workshop I glued it over a level concrete floor with No Nails glue, thus making the floor more user friendly to dropped tools, cold feet, sliding furniture projects and machines.

HARDBOARD
This is made from wood fibre pulped in water, and pressed at high temperature and pressure into thin, rigid boards. There are various grades, some oil tempered, some double faced, but the one in general use has one hard, smooth and shiny side while the other has a weave-like textured surface.

I use this to cover bench tops and tool tables to provide a cheap, smooth, hard-wearing, replaceable surface. It is also very useful for rods, jigs, marking out, bases and backs in workshop drawers, storage boxes and cupboards.

MDF

MDF printer stand, stained mahogany colour.

Drawer with cedar of Lebanon casing, plus base in cedar-faced MDF.

Now popular with furniture makers, MDF is made in a similar way to hardboard but at lower temperature and pressure. It has no grain direction, the edges do not need to be lipped and they can be moulded just like solid wood.

MDF is stable and ideal for veneering purposes as it is cheaper than ply, and heavier. It is, however, not as strong, particularly in curved applications. I buy it in pre-veneered sheets for use in cabinet backs and drawer bases, where, because of its stability and lack of movement, it can be glued into a carcass all round to give great rigidity.

I used some thicker non-veneered pieces to make a stand for my scanner and printer, which I stained mahogany and varnished. It is acceptable as a workaday item, and was quick and easy to make up.

PLY

Plywood is made up from thin sheets of wood glued together, each layer having the grain direction at right angles to the layer on either side. This gives great strength and rigidity – in fact, weight for weight, plywood is stronger than steel. It was first used in the seventeenth century, but came into its own at the end of the nineteenth century, when it was manufactured in great quantities for tea chests.

I use pre-veneered sheets in similar circumstances to MDF for larger drawer bases and cabinet backs where greater strength or rigidity is required, and I prefer it to MDF in curved applications. It comes in a range of thicknesses and I have used modelmaker's $\frac{1}{16}$in (1.5mm) three ply for making small compartments, and the thicker stuff for chair seat bases.

BLOCKBOARD

This is really a form of ply but the centre core layer is thicker strips of solid wood, with veneer sheet bonded on each side. It is stable and has greater strength along the line of the grain of the centre core. The solid core also allows normal joints to be used. I picked some up on special offer once and made a small wardrobe from it, thinking that as it was pre-finished it would be quick. It wasn't – and I did not enjoy the making or the result much. All the edge lipping was finicky and the surface very unforgiving to any sanding. I prefer solid wood!

Ash-veneered blockboard wardrobe.

CONDITIONING AND HOME KILNING

A kiln or conditioning cabinet can be made from an airtight box lined with polythene, with a home dehumidifier to remove the moisture. The dehumidifier should be set to the manufacturer's recommended level for domestic interiors, and the water it removes from the inside air piped out. The wood must be air-dried and seasoned first to allow as much water as possible to be removed.

CHECKING MOISTURE CONTENT

Assume thoroughly air-dried wood has a water content of 20% by weight. Weigh a test piece and mark its weight on it. After about a month in the 'kiln', re-weigh the test piece. When it has lost around 8% of its original weight it will be about ready. The same cabinet can be used to condition kiln-dried timber for a week or two as a precaution.

STORING TIMBER

Once timber leaves the kiln it starts to adjust its moisture content to its surroundings, so it must be stored in conditions as close as possible to those it will end up in as a piece of furniture. Don't, therefore, keep it in a damp garage, or even a dedicated timber store, if it is not dry.

If the storage temperature and moisture conditions are close to those of the end use, you can store your timber with sticks between the boards, allowing free air flow to condition it.

Make sure the sticks are lined up directly over each other so that the weight is borne through the sticks and the boards are not deformed. If the storage conditions are not as dry as the end use conditions, store the boards flat on top of each other, with no air gap, and cover with a waterproof sheet to minimize the moisture intake.

Timber ends, one stick nailed and two painted to slow moisture loss from end grain and prevent splitting during drying.

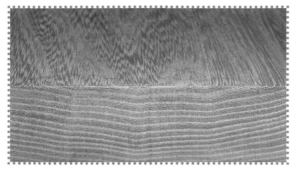

Tangentially sawn table top end – not stable.

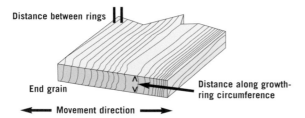

Quarter-sawn table top end – stable.

MOISTURE MOVEMENT

Most movement occurs when the moisture content is reduced from air-dried to a level for interior furniture use, and vice versa. The movement is across the grain but, for our purposes, not along it. Movement along the growth rings is twice that between them, making quarter or radially-sawn wood more stable than tangentially sawn. Wood will always move if its moisture content changes, and it will always try to equalize its moisture content to its surroundings.

The level of moisture in the air varies from summer to winter, and warm summer air holds more water. Cold air holds less water, but when centrally heated it can absorb more from its surroundings. The change of moisture content of the air causes solid wood furniture in normal domestic central heating to move from summer to winter. It tends to slowly swell in summer and shrink in winter. I usually allow for about ⅛th movement per 12in (305mm) of width of board across the grain in normal conditions. Wood moves across the grain but splits along it.

MOVEMENT IN QUARTER-SAWN TIMBER

Small amount of growth-ring circumference included, movement fairly even and at right angles to the faces, minimizing distortion

MOVEMENT IN TANGENTIALLY SAWN TIMBER

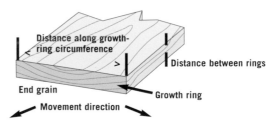

Little movement in the thickness of the board, i.e. between the growth rings, but a lot of movement along the circumference, causing the board not only to shrink but to distort or 'cup'. Minimum shrinkage on short, inside ring and maximum on outside causes 'cupping' in opposite direction to curve of rings

GROWTH-RING MOVEMENT

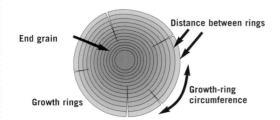

Movement is twice as much per inch along circumference as between growth rings. More shrinkage on the long outside rings causes checks and cracks

KILN

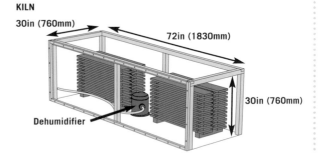

Airtight box – measurements to suit. Line with polythene to complete air-and damp-proofing. Front screwed onto foam draught excluder strip to seal. Condensed water piped to outside

FIXINGS AND FITTINGS
Screws
It has been said that a cheap screw is a waste of time, and can have serious consequences.

I use the Screwfix range of Posidrive turbo screws. The quality is excellent, delivery quick, and the price is right. They are hardened to prevent shearing and cam out of the head, and plated, which means no black staining when used in oak. I use mainly No.8 gauge (3.5mm) and keep a full range of lengths from ⅜–3in (10–75mm).

I also have a special box of hinge screws that includes a set of reduced-head screws. These can be a lifesaver in piano hinges, or any hinges where countersinks are too shallow.

Cabinet fittings
When it comes to specialist cabinet fittings the *Häfele Furniture and Hardware Fittings* catalogue is my bible – if they haven't got it then I don't want it.

There is an unbelievable range of fittings and decorative hardware for cabinets, and all sorts of domestic and office furniture. Detailed measurements and fitting instructions are given in the catalogue.

The company's agricultural ironmongery volume includes a similar range of big stuff for butch outdoor work.

SECONDARY MACHINING
Wood is constructed of fibres, pulling in slightly different directions but balancing each other out. When the wood is sawn or planed some of the fibres are cut, releasing the pull they were exerting, and allowing the remaining fibres to pull the wood into another shape.

The release of stresses is usually relatively short term in seasoned timber, and the wood stablizes quickly. Some of the stresses can be taken out by stretching the remaining fibres, so to minimize the distortion leave it overnight or longer in a warm dry place, to settle on stickers or under a weight.

WORKSHOP CONDITIONS
A warm, dry workshop is a prerequisite to serious cabinet making and safe, good-quality work. The workshop environment should be as close as possible to that which the finished item will live in, so it conditions while you work. There is little point in buying expensive kiln-dried timber, and working it accurately into a wonderful piece of furniture if the workshop conditions are spoiling it by the minute.

My workshop has vapour barriers to the walls and ceiling, insulation, draft-proofing, heating and a dehumidifier, as does my wood store. Furniture making isn't rocket science but the characteristics of the basic materials must be taken into account for good furniture, contented makers and happy clients.

Range of Posidrive stainless steel screws, and box of hinge screws some with reduced heads, dowel screws, brass screws, and a range of magnetic Posidrive bits, hinge centring bits.

Dehumidifier in loft timber store.

TIMBER SELECTION AND PREPARATION

It's all about the wood

Timber selection and preparation is a vital part of the making process. Time and care spent on this stage will be rewarded later on.

Checking for square on a hand-planed edge; preparation prevents poor wood performance.

The wood means everything in my furniture – its selection and preparation is the most important part of my making process. I take great care in the initial selection at the timber yard, subsequent storage, cutting out and allocation of specific pieces to the various component parts. Virtually all the serious thinking and decisions which affect the final outcome occur at this stage, so time spent here is seldom wasted.

CHOICE OF SPECIES

Different species have different characteristics, which may be relevant to the function of the piece. Is it a hard-working kitchen table or a hardly touched display cabinet? I would not recommend burr elm for a whole dining chair – it is too unpredictable and may have little tensile strength in the legs, although I might put a burr panel in the back. The client, in my experience, chooses mainly by colour, figure and texture of finish. They should be steered to a selection of timbers suitable for the job. To that end, our home is furnished with a wide range of my furniture in different timbers with natural finishes, each appropriate to its task. I find simple lines in natural oak, sycamore and ash most popular, with mahogany, dark oak and even burr elm less so.

AT THE YARD

The timber yard is where it all begins – a bad choice here guarantees a bad result. There is no definition of quality in wood – you get what is available in that yard at that time, so be prepared to invest time checking out other sources until you are happy. The amount of usable timber per board differs from species to species. One would expect consistent, clean boards with very few defects in American white oak, but a few more flaws in English oak. However, the American timber would have less figure and character. In a burr elm board the loss from defects, in-growing bark, large knots and faults, may be considerable. Imported hardwoods are generally of good quality with no wany edge or sapwood and, although more expensive per raw cube of material, have less waste, and can be more economical.

Kiln-dried wood will have been carefully controlled in its initial drying, making it more stable in the future. However, its current moisture content depends on how long it has been out of the kiln and how it has been stored. See previous chapter for more details.

With experience you will learn to recognize good quality in any specific timber species. Check each face of each board. Make sure they are over the nominal thickness and not tapered in the width, allow for end shakes, knots and other defects. The first few inches of each end of most boards are subject to splitting and should be marked out.

I buy the timber for each project as far in advance as possible. As soon as it gets into my clutches it is always stored properly, stacked flat on sticks in warm and dry conditions. The same applies during making and when work is left overnight or at weekends. This helps to prevent uneven drying and distortion.

Laburnum oysters conditioning under pressure.

Marked out board – note split ends and sapwood.

Checking for wind.

Partially prepared stock conditioning in the wood store.

Sapwood and wany edges.

CUTTING LIST

My first action in the process of making is to make a rough sketch with relevant measurements, onto the white board in the workshop. I then begin to list all the pieces and decide on the sizes and jointing methods. This all starts out very rough and ready, and is tidied up as the details crystallize in my mind.

Doing this cutting list really helps me to get right into the project. I don't give cutting lists in my published projects because any change in measurements or methods makes them redundant – far better for the person making the piece to do their own, and make their own decisions as they go.

PLANNING

Planning a logical sequence of making and assembly is critical to success. Where possible, all cuts of the same measurement should be made at the same time to utilize the same machine settings. The order of making component sub-assemblies is important. There is little point in having glued up a piece if it cannot be fitted to the carcass because other parts are already fitted and in the way.

MARKING OUT

The sawn timber is laid out in the workshop, both faces examined, defects marked and the best face chosen. I then begin to select individual areas of the timber for the relevant parts of the piece, marking them in chalk, allowing me to change my mind should I need to. I sometimes hand-plane a small area to check colour and figure but, by and large, I have learned to judge the look of a piece before it is planed up.

I choose the best-looking pieces for the most prominent areas of the finished piece. Boards which will be edge-jointed to make up a width are chosen to be of the same colour and complementary figure, preferably with the grain and figure running through the joint to disguise it. I like straight-grained timber for door frames (for stability and continuity), but nicely figured pieces for the panels. Where one face is seen and the other hidden, the best face is chosen for the outside, and the face with any blemishes put to the inside. Once I have made my choices, not forgetting to check the back of the board for any surprises, I start to cut to size.

Corrected marking out error.

Checking thickness.

Final accurate marking with a scalpel.

Checking ends are square.

ROUGHING OUT

Most of the timber I use is wany edged, through and through boards, which are often too wide to go over my planer and/or too long to rip on my tablesaw. I reduce the length by cutting on the radial-arm saw, which is set centrally between my two benches, so that long lengths are supported on each side.

Once the boards are cut to length, a reference edge is straightened on the planer and the individual pieces ripped to width on the tablesaw, or cut to the marked lines on the bandsaw. Of course, I leave extra length and width on these rough-cut pieces to allow for final accurate dimensioning, about 1in (25mm) on the length and/or the width of each piece.

SURFACING

The cut lengths are surfaced on the planer. If the piece is bowed at all, the hollow face is surfaced and ends swapped until the whole face has been in contact with the knives. I am careful not to put pressure on the board and bend it to the knives but let the machine take out the bow. If there is any wind in the piece, a saw-cut veneer of the correct thickness is glued to the rising corners to steady it as it goes over the knives, and the face planed. As soon as all the face has been in contact with the knives, I check that it is truly flat. If it has any bow, the thicknesser feed rollers will just press it flat while it is going through and it will spring back afterwards. Once I am sure it is true, I stop. I prefer to do as much stock removal on the thicknesser as possible, as it gives a better, more even finish.

THICKNESSING

I select the thickest-looking piece and set the table height to a slightly greater thickness so that the knives just clear the face, and pass the piece through, raising the table a little at a time until the knives just cut. At this setting, I pass all the pieces through to make sure there are no hidden surprises, hovering over the stop button in case a rogue thicker piece goes through and jams the feed rollers. After the first run, I raise the table a little at a time, passing all the pieces through until they all are of the same thickness. I check the thickness carefully with a Vernier gauge on both edges to make sure the knives are parallel to the table. For more stock

removal, I alternate the faces to even out the amount taken off each. This is in case the moisture levels are not the same throughout the timber. If the moisture levels are different on each face, the wood may cup or warp.

EDGING

The planer fence is checked to be square to the table and a test piece run over. This is also checked to ensure the knives are parallel to the tables, and any necessary adjustments made. One edge of each faced and thicknessed piece is marked as the reference, choosing the hollow edge – i.e. where both edge ends touch the table, but the centre does not, if there is one.

All the pieces are carefully passed over the planer to true them up, then I hand-plane the edges to a finish and check by eye and try square that they are true along and across the grain and free from ripples.

I take a lot of trouble with this true edge, as it is the reference for the remainder of the dimensioning and much of the jointing.

CUTTING TO WIDTH

The ripsaw blade is checked to be square to the table and, using the reference edge against the ripsaw fence, I cut the pieces to width, allowing an extra ⅛in (3mm) or so for finishing. The edges are then finished to size in a similar way to the true edge, by a combination of edge planing on the surfacer and hand-planing to a finished, accurate size.

CUTTING TO LENGTH

I am careful to set up my radial-arm saw properly and find it an absolute boon when cutting pieces to accurate length. A stop on the fence ensures repeat cuts of exactly the same length, and an accurately set, sharp blade ensures the cut is true in the vertical and horizontal planes. I always do a test cut and adjust as necessary. I rarely have to adjust on the shooting board. Marking at this stage is done with a scalpel, and the test cut is measured twice to make sure I do not make repeat mistakes.

One easily made mistake is to not allow for the length of the tenons. Nowadays that is easily rectified with a bead joint, biscuits, or loose wafer tenons.

Checking blade square on bandsaw.

Deep-sawn piece that has 'cupped'.

Checking flatness of face.

Deep-sawn pieces sticked and clamped while they settle.

DEEP SAWING

To make up panels, especially for doors, I often deep cut and book match a nice piece. With care, I can deep cut a generous 1in (25mm) board to make a ³⁄₈in (10mm) door panel. The only problem with deep sawing is the tendency of the cut pieces to cup, especially in kiln-dried timber. This is because the inside core of the timber is dry but the outside faces have absorbed water, swelled and are in tension. As both faces have swelled together, the effect is balanced and the board remains true. When it is deep cut the drier core becomes one of the faces of each of the two new pieces, and there is nothing to balance the tension in the original outside face. This causes the wood to cup with the newly cut face being concave. This can sometimes be alleviated to some degree by misting the concave face with water and covering it with clingfilm before leaving it under a weight overnight. Drying the convex face in direct sunlight, with a hair drier or a combination of both methods can also achieve the desired result.

The correct thing to do is to scrap the piece, but this can be a difficult decision to take and sometimes these remedies work. If the cupping is not too pronounced the board may be held flat in its eventual frame, and it may be possible to clamp or pin it flat temporarily, while the faces are finished.

Once I have deep-sawn any panels, I keep the pieces in clamps until I am ready to use them and get them made up, finished and into a frame as soon as I can.

DRAWER CASINGS

I usually have to deep saw cedar of Lebanon from 1in (25mm) thickness when making drawer casings. I have found it, almost without exception, free of any cupping at all, but I still cut the drawer pieces early on in the project and keep them sticked and stacked under a weight so that they can stabilize until I am ready to use them.

CONCLUSION

To me the essence of successful making is organization and planning. Good-quality timber should be bought in plenty of time, and looked after properly. An accurate cutting list should be made, a logical sequence of making planned and the right piece of timber selected for the right part of the project. Get all this right, and the furniture just makes itself!

WAYS OF JOINING WOOD
Joining Up

The key to successful joint making is to keep it simple and well made. Here are some of the most commonly used joints.

Hand-planing edges.

I don't go in for complicated joints if they are not necessary – rather a biscuit to reinforce a mitre than a secret dovetail – so here I will cover the main joints I use and keep things as simple as possible.

PRINCIPLES
Modern glues are very strong and make some of the more complicated traditional joints redundant, but there are some basic rules. The long grain, face or edge of a board, glues well to itself, but end grain will not glue to itself or to long grain. Clamping times and temperatures are vital, so read the instructions.

Make sure the joint is not 'starved'; as it clamps up. I like to see a nice consistent line of glue oozing from the joint. Remove this with a damp cloth while wet or with a scraper when hard. The hardened glue is not kind to keen-edged planes and chisels. Properly executed glue joints should be at least as strong as the wood, and any break or split should not be along the glue line.

LONG-GRAIN JOINTS
This is a simple joint, but one of the most important to get right. It can be used to glue edge to face and face to face as well as edge to edge, provided the grain is running in the same direction. I use it for cabinet panels, table tops and door panels etc.

Once the timber for a project has been prepared, I join up all the pieces to width. The narrow pieces are laid out and the best face selected to match figure and colour - I try to arrange the figure to run through the glue line to mask it.

The faces and edges are marked, and the edges planed square on the surface planer. To compensate for any slight inaccuracy in the setting of the planer fence, I reverse the face of alternate boards presented to it. The boards are laid out flat again and the edges checked for a good fit. Each edge is then hand-planed to remove the planer ripples and a couple of strokes extra are taken off the middle of each, so that when placed together again there is a slight gap or hollow at the centre of the glue line. When the joint is clamped at the centre, the ends draw up tight as the joint closes. The pressure on the ends also helps prevent any splits caused by extra drying out from the end grain, which loses moisture more readily than long grain.

CLAMPING

This should take place on a flat, level surface with all the clamps clean and set to the right size. Hardened glue on the clamp bars can mark the work, and can impede free movement on the screw threads. To stop glue sticking to the threads and keep them running free, I give them an occasional light spray with WD40.

Wooden blocks, battens, or padding should also be ready, if necessary, to prevent the jaws marking the work. Before spreading the glue I usually do a dry run, make sure the joints fit accurately and that everything is properly prepared.

At least three clamps are used, one at each end underneath, and one on top in the centre. This helps to prevent the clamps pulling the piece out of true. On longer pieces, more clamps are used; three under and two over, five under three over etc, allowing about up to about 18in (460mm) between clamps.

ADHESIVES

Aliphatic resin

My standard wood adhesive is Titebond Original from APT. A PVA-base with aliphatic resin additives, it is quick-grab, high-tack and cures quickly – its open time can be a bit short in warm weather on a long gluing-up job. Non-toxic, it can be cleaned up with water and dries a soft yellow. Suitable for wood, sheet materials, cloth, card and leather, it does not like low temperatures and is not a gap filler.

PVA

Another excellent glue for wood, it is more tolerant of low temperatures, does not have as fast an initial tack, and has a longer open time. It is ideal for a longer assembly job, where the extra open time is important, also a lack of initial grab allows pieces to slide more easily into position when clamped up. Suitable for sheet materials, leather, card and cloth, it is again not a gap filler.

There are many other adhesives available for more specialist requirements, some gap fillers, some waterproof and some instant fix, but these are the two I use for general, standard jointing.

Wafers on a long edge-to-edge joint. Self-guiding $^5/_{32}$in (4mm) router biscuit slot cutter used to cut slots.

PRESSURE

As the clamp pressure is applied, the under faces of the boards are kept flat on the clamp bars and the upper faces checked level with a straightedge. I use biscuits at each end and in the middle to prevent slip and keep the boards level to each other, as well as giving extra strength.

Wafers can be used as a continuous tongue, glued in to both boards for ultimate strength of the joint, and location of the pieces. This can help if you have a rough, twisty board.

Wafers are very useful as an easy way of making tongue-and-grooved edges where the joint is to be left dry to allow for movement, for instance an internal or external cottage door, or tongue-and-grooved panelling. Both edges are grooved with the router using a $5/32$in (4mm) cutter, the combined depths of the grooves being the width of the wafer +1mm, and wafers fitted dry, or glued into one groove only, thus allowing for movement across the grain without the joint opening right through.

STORAGE

When glued-up wide panels come out of the clamps it is important to remove any glue ooze and store them flat on sticks, in an appropriately warm, dry environment with free air flow to both faces, to help prevent warping. If possible, weight the top of the pile as well. Once in the constructed piece, other components will provide bracing to hold them flat.

BRACING WIDE PANELS

When bracing flat panels across the grain, allow for future movement of the wood. If the run of the grain in the bracing piece is the same as the panel, e.g. a shelf housed into a carcass side, then they should move together and can be glued. If the grain run on the brace is at right angles to that on the panel, e.g. braces across doors or under table tops, it should not be glued. I use screws for this type of joint.

DOUBLE COUNTERSUNK SCREW

I use this method on braces across relatively narrow opening solid wood tops. Braces, with plugged screws in double countersunk holes, are fixed across the underside of the lid to hold it flat, while the space around the screw still allows for movement across the grain.

Buttons and expansion plate shown under a table top.

Slotted brace for a table top.

Opening top brace fitted with double countersunk screws and holes then plugged.

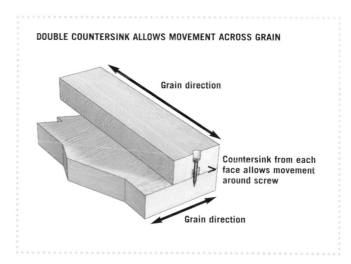

DOUBLE COUNTERSINK ALLOWS MOVEMENT ACROSS GRAIN

Grain direction

Countersink from each face allows movement around screw

Grain direction

SLOTTED SCREWS

Screws are driven through slots in the brace allowing movement across the grain. I use this for wider panels such as table tops, which may move more, relative to the frame.

OVERSIZE HOLES

When a plinth goes across the grain of the side of a cabinet, I glue the front end to the side to protect the mitre joint. I then drill an oversize hole through the back of the side to screw through to the plinth, supporting the screw with an oversize washer. This allows the side to move while holding the plinth securely in place.

HOUSINGS

These are also called grooves, slots, trenches and dados, so for our purposes the terms are interchangeable. Housing grooves were made in a variety of ways in the past. For example, a tenon saw to cut the edges and the waste removed with a chisel, or a special routing plane. Nowadays, we have the tremendous advantage of the router to make accurate grooves simply and quickly.

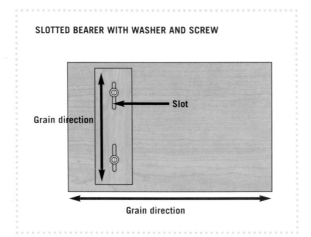

Cutting stopped housing.

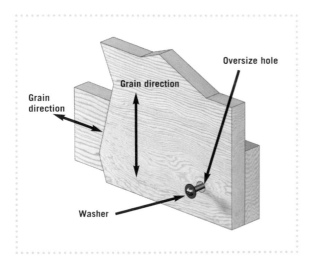

Adjusting shelf thickness for housing.

STOPPED HOUSINGS

For shelves and drawer frames I use a stopped housing, which is a slot usually cut across the grain – and stopped just short of the full width of the male component, meaning they do not show on the front edge of the receiving piece. I cut the slot with a router bit of the right size and squared the end with a chisel. A notch or shoulder is then cut on the front edge of the shelf or frame to allow entrance.

When the wood is thicknessed during preparation, it is left a bit 'fat' so that the end can be lightly sanded or planed to an exact fit in the slot. This form of housing joint should be a compression fit, and requires knocking home with a hammer and block.

The leading edge of the male piece can be very slightly bevelled to assist in starting the entry, the glue initially provides lubrication, then it swells the wood and, finally, gives some, if slight, grip. It is a mechanical joint; a sloppy fit relying on glue is ineffective.

Taken in isolation, most joints have a line of least resistance to force the direction of entrance for assembly – and this is particularly so in the case of this joint, because there is hardly any long grain to long grain glue area.

However, it provides enormous resistance to downward force – the wood would break before the joint. The line of least resistance is to a force pulling the shelf out of the slot and, in some cases, this can be countered by reinforcing with glue blocks or pocket screws. Other joints in the complete carcass construction should reinforce against this vulnerable direction.

Shelves clamped up into stopped housings.

Tapping shelf home into housing.

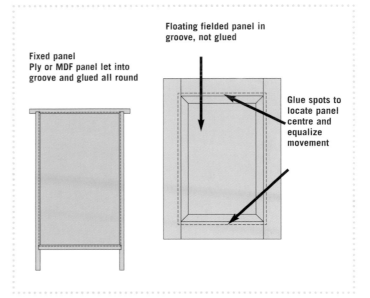

Fixed panel
Ply or MDF panel let into groove and glued all round

Floating fielded panel in groove, not glued

Glue spots to locate panel centre and equalize movement

PLAIN HOUSINGS

I use this joint to glue sheet material backs into cabinets and bases into drawers. It is light, simple and easy to execute, takes little space and gives enormous strength.

I measure the thickness of the sheet material with a Vernier gauge and select the next router cutter size down. The slot is cut about ¼in (6mm) in from the back edge and ¼in (6mm) deep. The sheet material is laid face down on the bench, and the back face is very slightly chamfered with a block plane or sanding block until it just fits the slot.

Glue is applied to the top inside edges of the slot and the sheet material is then tapped home. If the carcass has shelves or frames that reach to the back, I always try to glue and pin them to the back as well.

STOPPED HOUSING JOINT

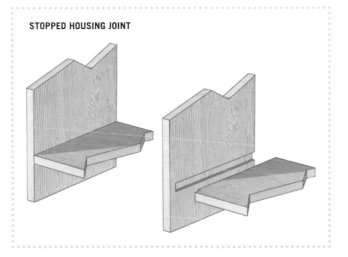

LOOSE PANELS

This is the reverse of the fixed panel. Here, the frame is bracing the panel that is held flat into the slots while being allowed to expand and contract across the grain in changing moisture conditions. I use this for doors, often with a fielded panel.

POCKET SCREWS

This joint has been brought into recent popularity by the introduction of some excellent jigs that make it easy to drill accurately. Housing, butt and biscuit joints can be greatly reinforced and do not need clamping while the glue sets. It has great 'pulling up' power and I have used it gratefully in circumstances where it was difficult or impossible to use a sash clamp. It is very important to set the depth of drilling carefully and use the correct screws. They are threaded half way up the stem, to bite only in the receiving piece, and have a flat head to locate properly on the base of the entry hole.

Tongue-and-groove boards across door, secret nailed to brace.

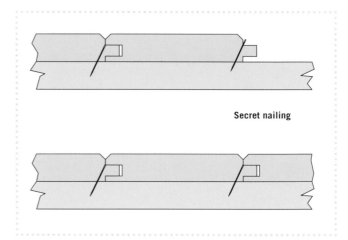

Secret nailing

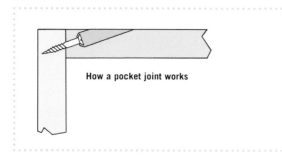

How a pocket joint works

Stopped housing and edge-to-edge joints reinforced with pocket screws.

A pocket hole joint on carcass work

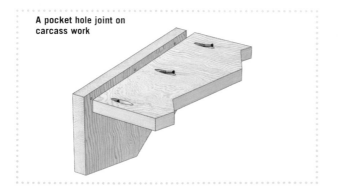

SECRET NAILING

This joint is used mainly on tongue-and-groove doors and floor boarding. The nail is driven at an angle through the tongue and is hidden by the groove of the next board.

CONCLUSION

Joining pieces of wood together is a fundamental requirement of furniture making and must be done properly. It is worth taking time to get it right. Use of machines, especially the router, has made it relatively easy to make good accurate joints, and modern glues make them strong and resistant to the normal – and abnormal – stresses put on a piece of furniture during its life.

STANDARD SOCKET JOINTS

I'm glad I joined up

Continuing with the subject of all things joined up, this section covers standard socket joints and the techniques used to make them.

Cutting a mortice with a router.

One of the basic requirements of our craft is to join prepared and shaped pieces of wood together to make a complete piece of furniture, and the means of achieving this are many and varied. Here, I will cover the standard socket joints I use most, and the techniques to make them. Of course, the joints may need modifying for special circumstances.

There are several jigs and guides that are available now and I make no apology for using them. If they make life easier and the job quicker I see no reason not to – providing there is no loss of quality.

BASIC PRINCIPLES
Joints must be carefully and accurately prepared, where possible do a dry check fit, and only glue and clamp up when you are sure of a good fit. Do not hope to force it together with the clamps!

Modern glues are very strong, but there are some basic rules. Long grain glues well to itself, creating a strong join, but end grain makes a weak join to itself or to long grain. Clamping times and also temperatures are important, so make sure to check the instructions. Glue is painted onto the inside faces of the socket and the faces of the tongue to ensure the joint is not 'starved', as it clamps up I like to see a nice, consistent line of glue oozing out. Properly executed glue joints should be at least as strong as the wood and any break or split should not be along the glue line.

MORTICE AND TENON
Essentially, this joint comprises of a socket in one piece into which a matching projection or tongue on the other is fitted. I mainly use the 'blind' version, where the mortice is not seen from the outside, in

frame construction – especially doors. The mortice should be about a third of the width of the thickness of the stile, approximately $\frac{1}{16}$in (1–2mm) deeper than the tenon length and the bottom at least $\frac{1}{4}$in (6mm) from the outside edge of the stile. The tenon tongue should be a sliding push fit and shouldered all round to control the depth of entry. My standard method is to cut the mortice to the correct depth with a router, using a cutter closest to the correct measurement. The ends are then squared off with a chisel or with the bench morticer. The tenon cheeks are usually cut on the radial-arm saw with a dado head, and the ends removed on the bandsaw to complete the all-round shoulder. I sometimes cut the whole joint on the bandsaw. In all cases, the tenons are cut 'fat' and trimmed with a shoulder plane to an exact fit. Tenons that are too thick are easy to adjust, those that are too thin are not!

Mortice and tenon joint cut on the Trend jig – note the rounded ends.

Beadlock joint.

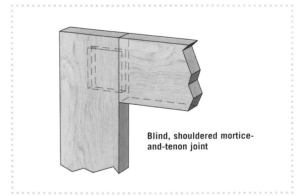

Blind, shouldered mortice-and-tenon joint

TREND MORTICE AND TENON JIG

Once set up accurately this is an excellent jig, ideal for material $\frac{1}{2}$–2in (12–50mm) thick and under 4in (100mm) wide. The material is clamped in the jig, and the mortices and tenons are cut using the correct cutters and bushes. The result is a perfect fit with rounded ends. The centre line setting is critical and it is wise to have a number of test pieces available to ensure the adjustments and measurements are exact.

Once the setup has been confirmed, cutting the joints is a quick and easy process – just make sure all the adjusters are tight to start with, and check at intervals during a long run, in case the vibration has loosened them. Square-ended joints can also be formed, but I have not found it necessary.

BENCH MORTICER

I use this occasionally for square stub mortices where the socket can be cut in one or two plunges; it is easier to use the router to cut longer mortices.

However, with the drill removed, the hollow chisel is extremely useful in squaring off the ends of router-cut sockets.

BEADLOCK JOINTS

This innovative loose-tongue joinery system from Trend is a very convenient, versatile, cost-effective jig, ideal for an occasional 'quickie'. Using the jig, a number of interlocking holes are drilled in each of the pieces to be joined, creating a mortice in each. The correct length of beadlock tenon dowel is then cut and glued into the mortices.

The shape of the mortice and the tenon/dowel maximizes the area of long grain-to-long grain contact, creating a very strong, accurate join. The different sizes of tenon dowel are available from Trend. A cutter is also available to make your own if you wish.

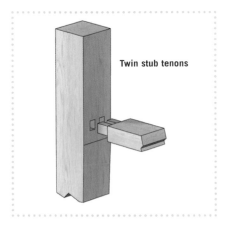

Twin stub tenons

VARIATIONS ON THE THEME

The mortice can go right through the piece so that the tenon end is visible – this is a much-favoured decorative feature on Arts and Crafts work.

Through and blind tenons can be wedged for strength and decoration, though I am not convinced of the advantage of wedged blind tenons, given the level of difficulty of making the wedge exactly right. A number of stub tenons create greater long grain-to-long grain contact than a single continuous tenon.

Tenons can be haunched to accommodate other joints or grooves, and can be pegged through one or both faces of the stile with a dowel for strength. On large pieces, such as beds or benches, the joint can be dry fitted and fixed with screws, bolts, or special fittings to create a 'knock-down joint'.

CORRECTING ERRORS

If a tenon is off-centre, it can be trimmed on the high side with a shoulder plane or bandsaw and a veneer of suitable thickness glued to the other; veneer can be glued to both sides of a tenon that is too loose. As a last resort, gap-filling glues can be used, but the curing time is several days. Do not fill the joint up with PVA and hope!

Beadlock kit showing lengths of tenon/dowel, drills, guide block and drill plate.

Double loose tenon joint using Tanseli wafers.

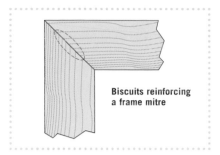

Biscuits reinforcing a frame mitre

BISCUIT JOINTS

I took ages to be convinced of the advantages of the biscuit jointer, but I would not be without one now. I recently purchased the king of them all – a Lamello S2 with the step memory height adjuster, enabling repeatable adjustments as fine as $\frac{1}{250}$in (0.1mm). I also use the glue applicators and they save a great deal of time.

The biscuit jointer is one of those machines that is sublimely simple and does what it's supposed to very well indeed with no accessories or complications – it cuts the right slot in the right place consistently and accurately.

I use biscuits in edge-to-edge joints to prevent slip when clamping up, and to reinforce butt, frame and mitre joints. Double biscuits can be used in material over $\frac{3}{4}$in (11mm) thick. Remember that the same rules of gluing apply. The biscuit surface is long grain and it should be glued to long grain in the slot. A biscuit glued to short grain in one slot can be used to locate, while a pocket screw is used to reinforce.

I also use Tanseli wafers as loose tenons where a biscuit would not be suitable. A biscuit jointer or a $\frac{5}{32}$in (4mm) cutter on the router can be used to cut the slot.

Close-up of double biscuit joint.

Through tenons with decorative contrasting wedges.

Post leg end used as decorative through stub tenon.

Cutting dovetails on a bandsaw.

I use two types; the through dovetail that is visible on both sides of a corner joint and the lapped joint that is visible on one face but hidden by a lap on the other, as in a drawer front. Apart from drawers, the other main use I have for dovetails is joining the top rail of a table frame or carcass to the leg or side where there is no room for a mortice.

Through dovetails are another favourite of Arts and Crafts furniture and can be used to decorative effect by forming a pattern of different sizes or spacing and taking advantage of the natural contrast of end and side grain, or by using contrasting timbers.

MITRE JOINTS

Where no end grain is to be seen in a joint between two pieces of timber, a mitre is required. If the pieces are of equal section, the mitre will halve the angle, otherwise it will need to be drawn across the joint from corner to corner, and the different angles on each piece measured and cut. I use mitres on cabinet plinths, frames and some table tops.

Biscuits or loose tongues, usually made from Tanseli wafers, are used for reinforcement. I use a strap clamp and blocks to pull up and hold the mitre while the glue sets. The outside edge on plinth mitres can be tapped over gently with a small hammer, to bring the fine fibres together in a perfect fit.

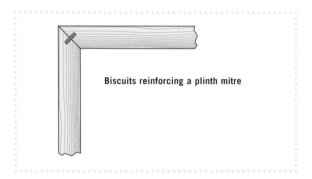

Biscuits reinforcing a plinth mitre

DOVETAILS

These are really an open mortice-and-tenon joint that incorporates a taper for extra mechanical strength. It is my favourite joint and I really enjoy making them by hand. To me and, I find, my clients, they epitomize handcrafted work and I do not use any machine jigs to produce them. That is not to say that I do not let the router and bandsaw take the strain by removing the bulk of the waste!

I mark the tails with a scalpel and cutting gauge. Using a template with a rake of 1 in 7, remove the bulk of the waste on the bandsaw and trim back to the line with a paring chisel. The socket is then marked using the tail as a pattern for the scalpel. The bulk of the waste is removed with the router, and final individual trimming is with a paring chisel.

HALF LAPS

Where two pieces of wood cross, a halved joint is much stronger than dowels or tenons. I make them on the radial-arm saw using multiple cuts, setting the blade depth to a tad less than half the thickness, and using stops to ensure accurate first and last cuts. The sides are cut to an exact fit on the saw, the base is trimmed down to size, and the saw cut marks taken out with a shoulder plane. I check the fit with a partial insertion and try to fully assemble the joint only once, after glue has been applied.

DOWELS

On small section pieces, it is often easier to use a dowel joint. Where possible I turn a dowel on the end of the piece using the lathe and a sizing tool. A hole is drilled in a piece of scrap with the drill bit to be used and test pieces turned until there is an exact fit, then the sizing tool set. I usually cut the shoulders on the radial-arm saw, setting the blade to the correct depth and using a stop fixed to the fence.

Proprietary loose dowels have grooves in the sides to allow air and surplus glue out when the joint is clamped up. On home-made dowels a kerf should be cut with a tenon saw along the length of the dowel. There are various jigs available for marking and drilling dowels accurately. I use the Trend mortice and tenon jig, or some proprietary false dowels with centre pins fitted to the holes drilled in one piece. When the joint is lined up and gently pushed together, leave a centre mark for the drill bit.

Where one face of the dowelled joint will not be seen, I usually drill right through both pieces to the correct depth and trim the end of the dowel flush rather than make a hidden dowel. I usually use plugged screws. I have several combined drill, countersink and plug cutter sets to do this easily.

This is not a comprehensive list of all the joints in furniture making, only the basic versions of those I mainly use. It doesn't matter how the joint is achieved – only that it fits, is appropriate to the loads on it, is glued and clamped properly and can be made in a reasonable time. Joints are the means to the end – not an end in themselves.

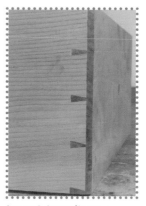

Fitting a bun foot with a dowel and screw dowel.

Lapped dovetails on a drawer front.

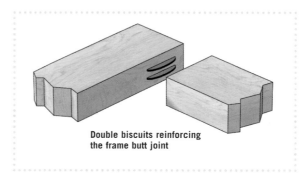

Double biscuits reinforcing the frame butt joint

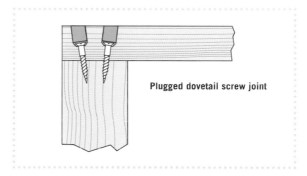

Plugged dovetail screw joint

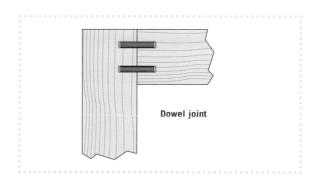

Dowel joint

Turning an end dowel using a sizing tool.

Mahogany Filing Cabinet

Oak China Cabinet

Chest of Drawers in Pale Ash

Bedside Tables in Pale Ash

Oak Settle

Oak Television Cabinet

Reception Desk in Sycamore

Burr Elm Apothecary's Chest

Oak Counter

Oak Desk

MAHOGANY FILING CABINET
Brazilian Beauty

Legal and sustainable Brazilian mahogany is not quite as easy to find as it used to be, which I discovered when making this versatile filing cabinet.

The finished piece in all its glory.

My client on this commission likes unusual timbers and contrasting combinations and so do I – we have had a long and enjoyable relationship. The original commission of this set was a large partners' desk in this style and combination of timbers. Subsequently, a large and matching glazed bookcase was ordered, and now the set was to be extended by the addition of this filing cabinet.

SPECIFICATIONS

The requirement was for a two-drawer filing cabinet to take standard suspension files sliding from front to back on metal bearers. The load in each drawer would be heavy, so full extension ball-bearing metal runners would be necessary to allow the drawers to open easily and fully. The height and width of the cabinet was dictated by the file size and the client specified a depth of $22\frac{1}{2}$in (572mm). The finish, to match the previous two pieces, was to fume and oil the mahogany and use a satin, water-based varnish on the cherry to preserve its pale contrasting colour.

TIMBER SELECTION

For the previous pieces, made some years ago, I chose Brazilian mahogany *(Swietena macrophylla)*, which was fairly readily available then, but has recently become more expensive and harder to source. I found some, at a price, through my local joinery supplier, who held a reasonable range of sizes. This meant I could buy with little waste, and the timber was certified from a sustainable and legal source. I was also able to get some good quality English cherry *(Prunus avium)* for the drawer fronts.

TIMBER PREPARATION

The components were marked out, cut oversize and left for some weeks to settle in the timber store, where a dehumidifier is used to help dry timber. Final conditioning takes place during making in the workshop, which is also kept at optimum conditions with a dehumidifier and sawdust burner. To avoid movement, the relative humidity levels in the workshop and timber store should be kept as close as possible to the conditions the piece will finally live in. Weekend makers should not leave it in a cold, damp garage all week. It could be brought inside, perhaps to a spare bedroom.

Brazilian mahogany

This is currently the best replacement timber available for the legendary Cuban or Spanish mahogany, which was used in period furniture for more than 200 years. Both are no longer commercially available due to its indiscriminate exploitation. It seems that Brazilian mahogany will unfortunately go the same way. The timber normally comes in straight-edged boards with little of the pale sapwood. The heartwood, when first planed in the workshop, can look pale pink but its light brown to deep brown-red characteristic colour is quickly brought out by age, exposure to light and air, fuming and finishes such as oil. It's moderately easy to work, having a fairly straight grain, though occasional interlocked pockets, which tend to tear, require a careful approach with a sharp, finely set plane or scraper. It finishes to a medium texture with some nice figure and there is not much movement in use.

English cherry

This is a straight-grained, fine-textured, pale straw-brown timber. Sometimes it can have a green streak along the grain like elm. The brown of the heartwood has a pink tinge – an ideal colour to match the red of the fumed mahogany. It finishes to a fine silky surface but can chip badly on the cross-grained patches. It tends not to season well and is subject to splitting and warping, causing high wastage. This increases its price, and it is wise to view the timber before purchase. American cherry is a completely different timber and is darker, redder and cheaper!

Cutting biscuit slots in the plinth mitres.

CONSTRUCTION

The top

The top was made up to width from three pieces, $^7/_8$in (22mm) thick, carefully selected for the best matching figure and colour. They were edge-jointed with biscuit reinforcement, clamped up and left to set. Then cut to exact size, checked for squareness and routed with a $^1/_4$ x $^1/_4$in (6 x 6mm) stopped housing underneath the rear edge to take the ply back. The $^7/_8$ x $^1/_4$in (22 x 6mm) stopped housings were routed for the sides, and the ends squared off with a chisel. The top and bottom of the edges were rounded over with a radius router cutter.

The sides

The sides were made up in a similar way to the top, from $^7/_8$in (22mm) stock, cut to exact size and checked for square. A $^1/_4$in x $^1/_4$in (6 x 6mm) slot was cut in the rear edge to take the ply back, biscuit slots were cut to take the crossrails and plinth backing strip, and shoulders cut on the tops and bottoms, front and back, to fit into the stopped housings in the top.

Crossrails

The crossrails and plinth backing strip were cut to length on the radial-arm saw and biscuit slots cut in the ends. A pocket screw slot was cut in the centre of the bottom face of the lower rails, the top face of the upper rails and back face of the backing strip.

Back and plinth

The back was cut to size from a sheet of mahogany-faced ply. I prefer ply or MDF for backs as it does not move, meaning it can be glued into the slot all round. This adds great strength to a carcass, especially against 'racking'. The plinth pieces were cut to length and thicknessed down to $^5/_8$in (16mm). A moulding was cut on the top edges using an ogee cutter on the router table. The radial-arm saw was carefully set and, after a trial run on a piece of scrap, the mitres were cut on the plinth corners.

I use a biscuit in such mitres, as it not only adds strength but also stops 'slip' when clamping up. Be careful to get the position of the biscuit correct – I have had the edge of a biscuit appear through the face when sanding. I carefully set the biscuit jointer, and made a test cut in an offcut from the plinth stock, before cutting the slots in the mitre faces.

CARCASS CONSTRUCTION

Titebond was applied to all of the biscuit slots in the sides, and the crossrail and plinth backing strip ends. The biscuits were fitted and the rails and backing strip clamped into position in the sides. The diagonals were measured and adjusted until all was square. The pocket screws were driven home in the top and bottom rails. One can then leave the carcass on a flat level surface to set. Next, the ply back was check fitted dry by springing it into the slot in the sides. It was then removed, the position of the middle back crossrail marked on the side edges, glue applied into the slot, and the back edge of the back crossrails and the back refitted.

When it was in position, I checked the carcass for square, making any necessary adjustments, and pinned the back to the glued surface of the rails.

All clamped up.

UPSIDE DOWN

I placed the top upside down on a piece of carpet, and applied glue to the stopped housings for the sides and back. The carcass was dropped onto the top, the sides and back located in their stopped housings and tapped in using a rubber hammer.

I lifted the whole unit up and placed it, top down, on my Workmate and applied the clamps. I clamp tops upside down where possible to stop any glue ooze. The front piece of the plinth was glued and screwed through the backing strip into position. The biscuit slots in the mitre and the mitre itself were glued, biscuits fitted and the plinth sides strap clamped.

The first 3in (75mm) of the plinth sides were also glued and screwed to the sides again from the back. The remainder of the plinth sides were left dry. They were fixed at the back from the inside through an oversize hole with a screw and washer. This allowed for movement across the grain of the sides. The mitres were tapped over and sanded to finish when dry. Once the plinth had set, strengthening blocks were glued under the bottom crossrails.

DRAWER FITTING

The drawer runners were supported on a piece of ply on the inside of the carcass half way up the drawer side, and screwed in (see box opposite). A strip of veneer was taped on top of the carcass crossrails and the drawer fitted into position. I pulled it out a little and screwed the bearer to it using the adjustment slots, as they were visible. Once the bearers were attached the veneer was removed to give clearance. Using the leeway given by the fixing slots, the drawers were adjusted. I drove the screws through the holes in the bearers to prevent movement.

Cutting the slots in the sides for the carcass rails.

In close up... the runners showing adjustment slots and fixing holes.

FUMING

All the surfaces had been finished before assembly with belt and orbital hand-sanders down to 240grit. I carefully checked for marks and glue ooze and, finally, hand-sanded down to 320grit.

I then made a frame using ¾in (19mm) plastic overflow pipe and fittings bought from a builders' merchant. I covered it in thin polythene sheet, to form a fuming tent. The pipe comes in 10ft (3048mm) lengths with a range of fittings, and is a cheap way of making a large temporary chamber that takes up little storage. It can also be used in with a dehumidifier, as a temporary conditioning tent.

I put plastic tubs of ammonia 890 in the tent and weighted down the edges of the sheet to the floor with strips of wood to make it airtight. Gloves and eye protection were worn – concentrated ammonia is toxic and causes damage to eyes on contact.

DRAWER CONSTRUCTION

The construction of the drawers was different from my normal method as they were on metal runners. The sides were inset by ½in (12mm) to allow space for the runners and were thicker to take the runner fixing screws. To allow for the inset, I glued a strip, cut from across the board so that the grain direction matched the drawer side, onto the front edge, where the dovetails would be cut. The length of this strip was the same as the length of the dovetails. The depth of the lapped dovetail in the drawer front was cut deeper than the drawer side thickness, leaving room for the runner between the drawer side and the carcass side.

All the pieces for the drawers were cut to size, fitted and marked. The sides were slotted for the bases and taped together, the top one marked and the tails cut out on the bandsaw. The fronts and backs were marked from the tails, and the waste removed with the T5 router. Each joint was finished with a chisel.

Blind slots were cut in the fronts and backs to take the ⅛ x ⅝in (3 x 16mm) stainless steel file bearers, and the drawer was assembled with a mahogany-faced MDF base glued in all round. It was glued and pinned at the back, and the drawer checked for square and wind, and left to set. Meanwhile, I turned the pulls on the lathe from scrap.

DRAWER FINISH

The cherry-fronted drawers were not fitted while the carcass was in the tent, as a test had established that cherry turns a deep golden brown if fumed. Instead, the fronts were finished with three coats of Aquacote acrylic satin varnish to keep a lighter contrasting colour. This was applied with a paint pad and cut back between coats. The remainder of the drawer carcass was then lightly waxed.

CARCASS FINISH

I chose Danish oil finish for the mahogany to really enhance its deep red/brown colour. I liberally applied a first coat of oil diluted 50/50 with white spirit, and renewed every hour or so for a day until the wood would take no more. Then I removed all surplus oil to prevent any build up on the surface, and left it to dry and harden in my warm, dry workshop for 24 hours.

This surface was cut back by hand with a 320grit paper on a sanding block, followed by a light coat of oil every 24 hours for a week. It was cut back between coats with a Scotchbrite grey pad. Ten days was then allowed for final hardening.

CONCLUSION

The other pieces of this set were made a few years ago, when sourcing Brazilian mahogany was not a problem. I was surprised at its scarcity and expense when I bought some for this project. Perhaps this means that conservation is working, but I suspect that the illegal stuff may just be going 'elsewhere'.

Cutting out the deep dovetails on the bandsaw.

Fuming inside polythene tent.

Brazilian Beauty

Solid top

Planted on 'double' dovetails

Veneered bottom

Veneered back

Sides housed into top

Pocket screws for top and bottom rails

Carcass rails

Solid sides

Rear fixing of plinth with screw and washer through over-size hole to allow for movement

All carcass joints biscuited

The drawers partly opened showing the metal runners.

Without the drawers. Carcass crossrails and drawer runners are clearly visible.

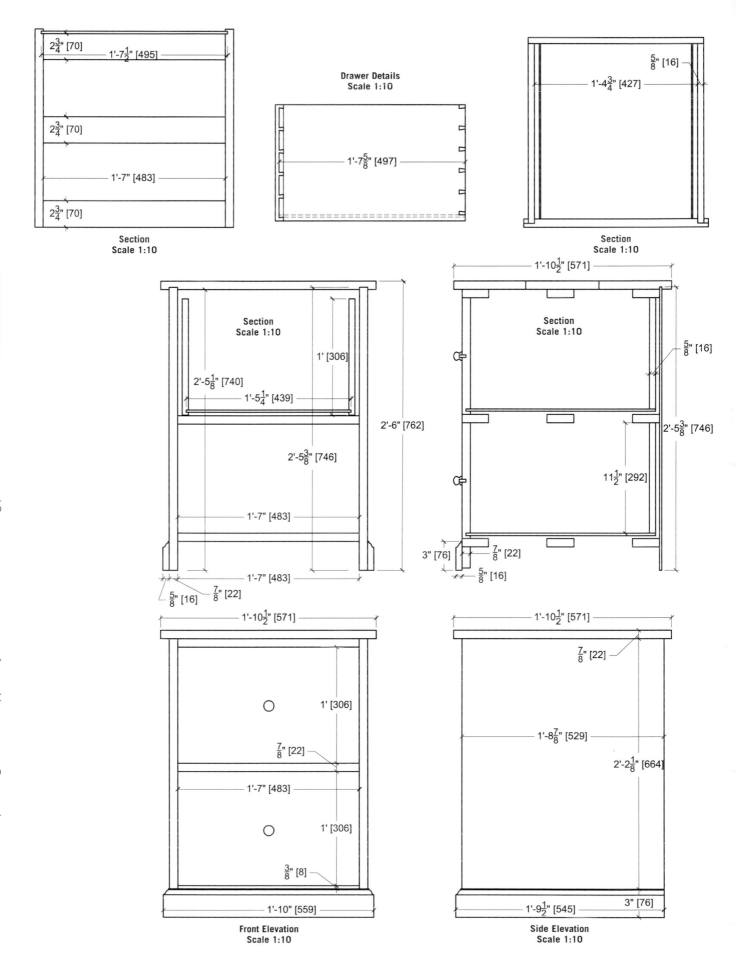

2¾" [70]

1'-7½" [495]

2¾" [70]

1'-7" [483]

2¾" [70]

Section
Scale 1:10

Drawer Details
Scale 1:10

1'-7⅝" [497]

⅝" [16]

1'-4¾" [427]

Section
Scale 1:10

Section
Scale 1:10

1' [306]

2'-5⅛" [740]

1'-5¼" [439]

2'-5⅜" [746]

2'-6" [762]

1'-7" [483]

1'-7" [483]

⅝" [16]

⅞" [22]

1'-10½" [571]

Section
Scale 1:10

⅝" [16]

2'-5⅜" [746]

11½" [292]

3" [76]

⅞" [22]

⅝" [16]

1'-10½" [571]

1'-10½" [571]

⅞" [22]

1' [306]

⅞" [22]

1'-7" [483]

1'-8⅞" [529]

2'-2⅛" [664]

1' [306]

⅜" [8]

1'-10" [559]

1'-9½" [545]

3" [76]

Front Elevation
Scale 1:10

Side Elevation
Scale 1:10

SEE PAGE 6 FOR NOTES ON USING PLANS

OAK CHINA CABINET

My Old China

Arts and Crafts and oak are two of my favourite things – so I was delighted with this commission.

The finished piece.

The order for this cupboard came from a family member with a keen interest in design in general, and furniture in particular. It usually makes me nervous establishing business relationships with friends and family, but his knowledge of design, wood, furniture and my work reassured me. He has always been drawn to Arts and Crafts furniture and, after a good rummage through my books on the subject to help in his design process, the piece began to take shape. The cupboard was to store china and had to fit into a specific space in his kitchen, so he had to juggle the overall size and the shelf settings to achieve maximum storage in a minimum space. This tapered tall cupboard, with an overhanging chamfered top, cutout front brackets from the top to the sides and simple feet, makes a nicely designed and balanced piece.

TIMBER

During a recent visit, this client, while in his other role as my brother-in-law, had been hijacked into helping me move a large piece out of the workshop for a photography session. The piece we were shifting was a counter in American oak and he liked the look of it so much he chose the timber for his own piece.

I was pleased, as American timbers are consistent, high quality and readily available. I went to my local joinery supplier and selected from a good batch of wide, 10ft (3m), straight-edged planks and had it delivered immediately.

I like to condition imported timber for a good while in the workshop, which is heated and dehumidified, because there is no telling know how long it has been since it was kiln-dried, or how it has been treated since.

CUTTING OUT

After it had been sticked and stacked for three weeks in the workshop, I began the marking and cutting out. As this was a tapered piece, I drew it full size on a piece of hardboard and took all the measurements, including the various shelf lengths, and the angle of tapered cuts, from the drawing.

I then chose a nicely figured piece for the door panels with matching pieces for the door frames and front carcass frame. The sides and top were chosen next, leaving the remaining timber for the base and shelves. The back was cut from a piece of ply, oak-faced on each side. All the timber, including the door panels, was cut slightly over length, and faced and thicknessed. The carcass pieces and door frames to a thickness of $7/8$in (22mm).

THE SIDES

A single board was cross-cut to length for each side on the radial-arm saw, having set the blade to the correct angle. A tenon was formed for the top, by making the side $\frac{3}{8}$in (10mm) longer than the front and back frames.

The shelf spacings marks were transferred from the front frame to the sides, and stopped housings $\frac{3}{8}$in (10mm) deep were cut for the shelves with a router. I loosened the slider plate on the router base and slipped in shims on one side to form the correct angle for the cut.

Housings were cut on the inside edges at the back of the sides for the oak-faced ply back to be glued in. Pencil marks for the centres of the shelf back edges were made on the back edge to aid pinning the back to the shelves.

CONSTRUCTION

The sequence of construction was to make the front frame, which would be laid on top of the sides, shelves and base, fix the top, and then fit the doors.

Using the long shank of drill bit to check angle on router. Note packing on router base to achieve the angle cut.

FRONT FRAME

Measurements for this frame were taken from the full size drawing. The stiles were cross-cut to length at the correct angle on the radial saw, the taper cut on the length made on the bandsaw and machine and hand-planed to exact size. Top and bottom rails were cut to length and width, also to the measurements on the drawing.

The bottom rail was joined to the stiles with a double biscuit joint – the top rail was too narrow for biscuits, so a double wafer joint was used instead. An angled cut below the bottom rails shaped the feet, and spacings for the shelves were marked on the front of the frame.

SHELVES

Carefully checking the measurements on the full-size drawing, I cut the shelves to length and then marked them clearly. They were check fitted to the stopped housings in the sides and a shoulder was cut on the front and back, at the correct angle, to overlap the stopped housing.

The shelf front edges were rounded over with a radius cutter on the router table. Pockets were drilled on the under face of the bottom shelf for reinforcing screws.

The carcass front bottom. Double biscuit joint.

Carcass front top. Double wafer joint.

Checking the angle of the taper on carcass.

Marking the front for shelves.

ASSEMBLY

The assembly sequence for this piece was to glue the shelves to the sides, biscuit the front frame onto the sides and shelves, then fit the top. The first clamping operation involved many joints with the added complication of the taper, so I decided on a dry run. Clamps and suitable battens were prepared, the shelves and sides dry assembled and diagonals checked to ensure the taper was even.

Finishing the inside of this cabinet would be difficult once the unit was assembled because of the close spacing and number of shelves. I decided to sand the shelves and the inside faces of the sides and back to a finish, and apply three coats of Aquacote satin acrylic varnish before assembly. Masking the ends of the shelves and the stopped housings protected the glue joints. Once the varnish had hardened off, I applied Titebond to the housings and clamped up for real. With the clamps in position, the reinforcing screws were driven into the pockets in the base. The back was glued into place and pinned to the shelf backs.

FITTING THE FRONT

Biscuit slots were cut in the front edges of the sides and corresponding slots in the inside faces of the front frame.

Biscuits were fitted dry and the front frame was offered up. With a little gentle persuasion it fitted, so it was removed, and the inside faces varnished, again with the glue areas masked off. Once the varnish cured, glue was applied to the biscuits, slots and edges of the sides, and the clamps fitted.

TOP

The top was cut to size and stopped housings cut to take the tenons formed by the ends of the sides protruding above the front frame. These tenons were at an angle, so the top edges were squared up to fit into the top mortices with a shoulder plane. Biscuit slots were cut in the top rail of the front frame, and corresponding slots in the under face of the top. A stopped housing was cut in the underside of the back edge to take the top edge of the ply back.

I marked the chamfer on the front and sides of the top in pencil and removed the majority of waste on the surface planer. This involved supporting the top at the correct angle against the planer fence, using the adjacent tablesaw fence to lift up and support one end. The top guard of the planer was removed and I did some trial runs with the machine off – if a guard is removed for a special operation, check it carefully to ensure safety. The chamfer was finished with a jackplane, scraper and sanding block. The top was then dry fitted, a pattern for the front brackets made in hardboard and the slots cut for their loose tenon wafers. I sanded the inside face of the top and finished with three coats of acrylic varnish. Once the varnish had hardened, glue was applied to the mortices, biscuits, biscuit slots and stopped housing for the back, and the top was clamped into position.

THE BRACKETS

Solid brackets are cut to size and shaped to fit between the side and the flat part of the top overhang, and check fitted. Slots for the loose tenons are cut in the brackets on the router table. The inside cutout is marked, a hole drilled to let the scroll saw blade in and the cutout made. I used a new blade to get as clean a cut as possible and minimize the finishing work on the internal faces.

Clamping the carcass.

FINISHING

Before fitting the brackets I completed the final power-and hand-sanding on the outside of the carcass, masked the small glue area of the brackets and finished the whole outside of the carcass with three coats of acrylic varnish. I hand-sanded the wood to 250grit and cut back the first grain – raising coat of varnish also with 250grit. Following coats were cut back with 320grit.

The brackets were finished separately at the same time and when all was dry, the masking tape was removed from the carcass, the brackets glued up and lightly clamped in to place.

DOORS

Stiles and rails for the door frames were cut to size. A single fielded panel in each door was the specification, but the thin stiles would flex, so I put an extra centre rail in at the back, out of sight, behind the panel. Double biscuit slots were cut at all the joints, the doors dry assembled, and the measurements for the fielded panels taken, allowing them to recess ¼in (6mm) into the frame.

The door panels were made up by deep sawing and matching some selected oak. The panels were cut to size and fielded using a vertical profile cutter on the router table, and the fieldings were finished with a shoulder plane, scraper and hand-sanding block. The panel faces were also sanded to a finish and all given three coats of varnish.

A slot was cut on the inside edges of the rails and stiles to take the panels, and the inside edges of the frames finished and varnished. The doors were assembled, glued and clamped, checked for square and wind, and left to set. The faces of the door frames were then sanded, and the completed doors fitted to the opening.

Brass butt hinges were fitted to the top, centre and bottom of the frames. All the brass door fittings were sanded and polished. The hinges were recessed fully into the door frame but not the carcass. All the brassware was removed from the doors and the frames sanded to a finish and given three coats of varnish.

Orbital sanding the top of the cupboard.

Removing the bulk of the waste for under fielding on planer.

Routing the angled stopped housings for the shelves.

HANDLES

My client wanted rectangular chamfered handles, so I shaped them on the radial-arm saw. I made multiple cuts on the ends of a 6in (150mm) piece of oak of the correct cross-section and cut the handles to length. The door hinges and catches were refitted and so were the doors. I made a careful check over the whole cabinet, cut back with a Scotchbrite grey pad and buffed to a nice sheen. I liked this cabinet, but I am always attracted to Arts and Crafts-style and oak. More importantly, my client liked it too.

My Old China

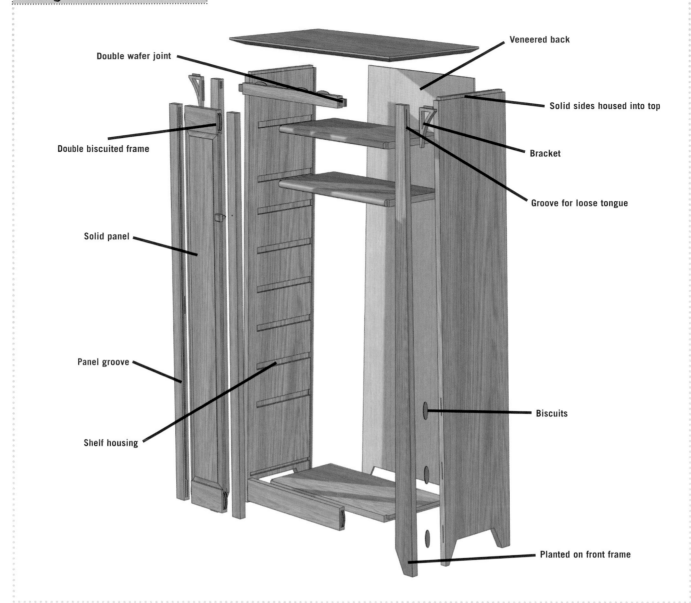

Double wafer joint

Veneered back

Solid sides housed into top

Double biscuited frame

Bracket

Solid panel

Groove for loose tongue

Panel groove

Biscuits

Shelf housing

Planted on front frame

The door pulls with screw dowel.

The top corner and bracket.

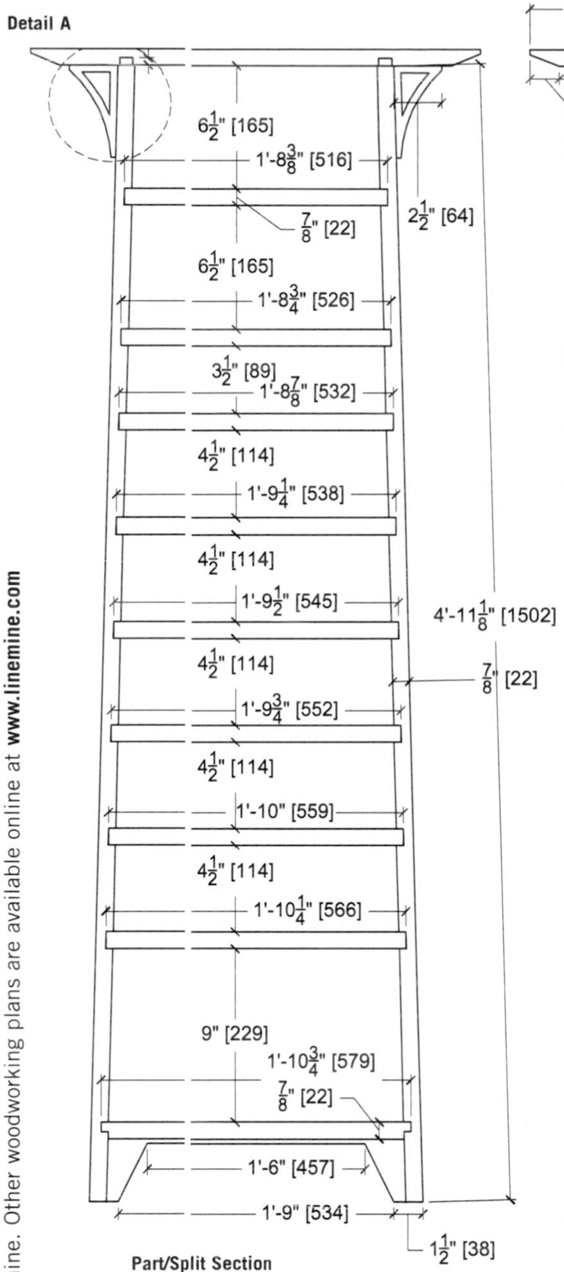
Detail A
6 1/2" [165]
1'-8 3/8" [516]
2 1/2" [64]
7/8" [22]
6 1/2" [165]
1'-8 3/4" [526]
3 1/2" [89]
1'-8 7/8" [532]
4 1/2" [114]
1'-9 1/4" [538]
4 1/2" [114]
1'-9 1/2" [545]
4'-11 1/8" [1502]
4 1/2" [114]
7/8" [22]
1'-9 3/4" [552]
4 1/2" [114]
1'-10" [559]
4 1/2" [114]
1'-10 1/4" [566]
9" [229]
1'-10 3/4" [579]
7/8" [22]
1'-6" [457]
1'-9" [534]
1 1/2" [38]

Part/Split Section
Scale 1:10

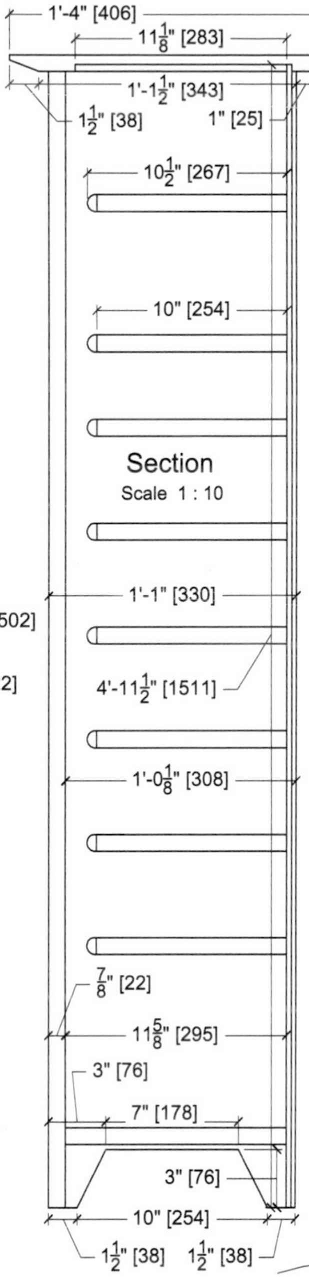
1'-4" [406]
11 1/8" [283]
1'-1 1/2" [343]
1 1/2" [38]
1" [25]
10 1/2" [267]
10" [254]
Section
Scale 1 : 10
1'-1" [330]
4'-11 1/2" [1511]
1'-0 1/8" [308]
7/8" [22]
11 5/8" [295]
3" [76]
7" [178]
3" [76]
10" [254]
1 1/2" [38]
1 1/2" [38]

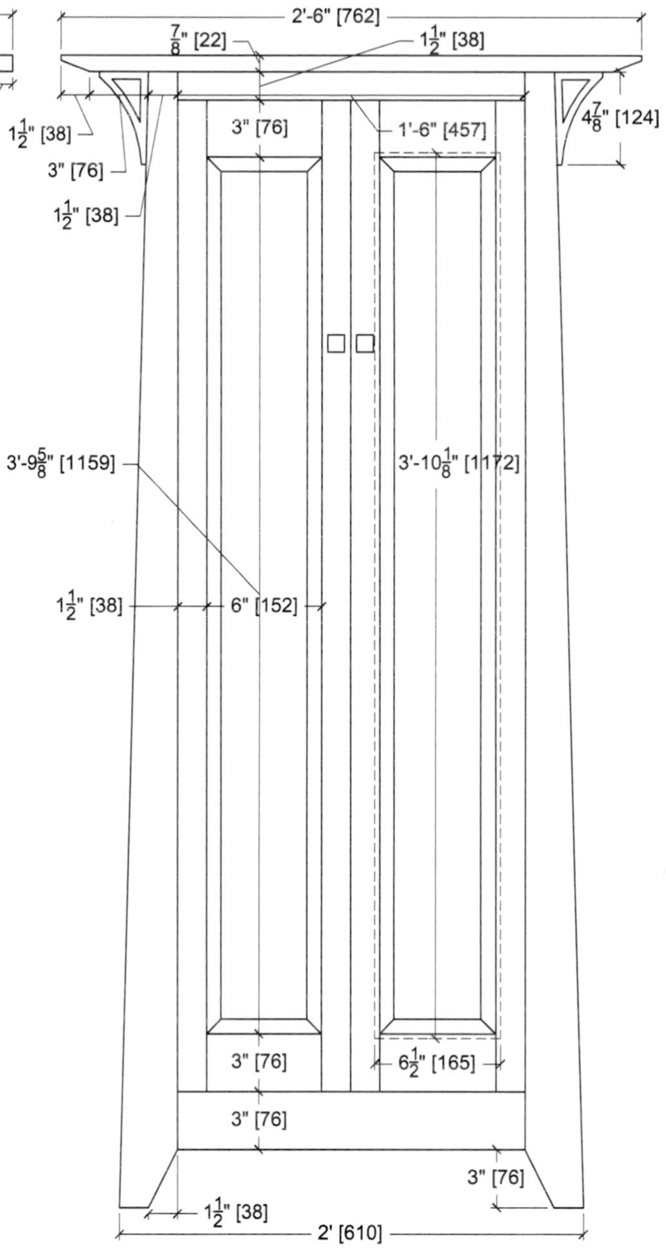
2'-6" [762]
7/8" [22]
1 1/2" [38]
1 1/2" [38]
3" [76]
1'-6" [457]
4 7/8" [124]
3" [76]
1 1/2" [38]
3'-9 5/8" [1159]
3'-10 1/8" [1172]
1 1/2" [38]
6" [152]
3" [76]
6 1/2" [165]
3" [76]
3" [76]
1 1/2" [38]
2' [610]

Front Elevation
Scale 1:10

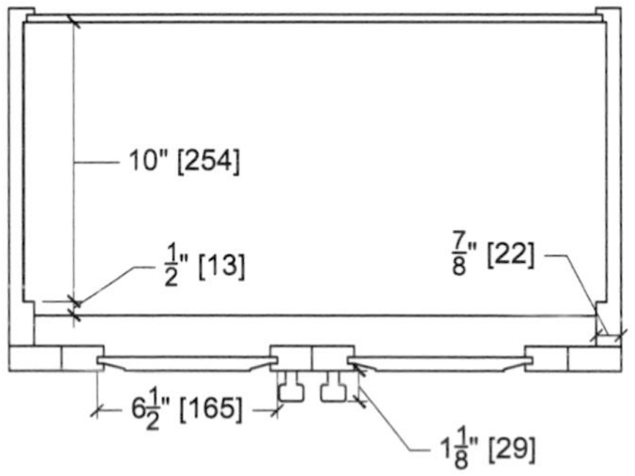
10" [254]
1/2" [13]
7/8" [22]
6 1/2" [165]
1 1/8" [29]

Plan Section
Scale 1:10

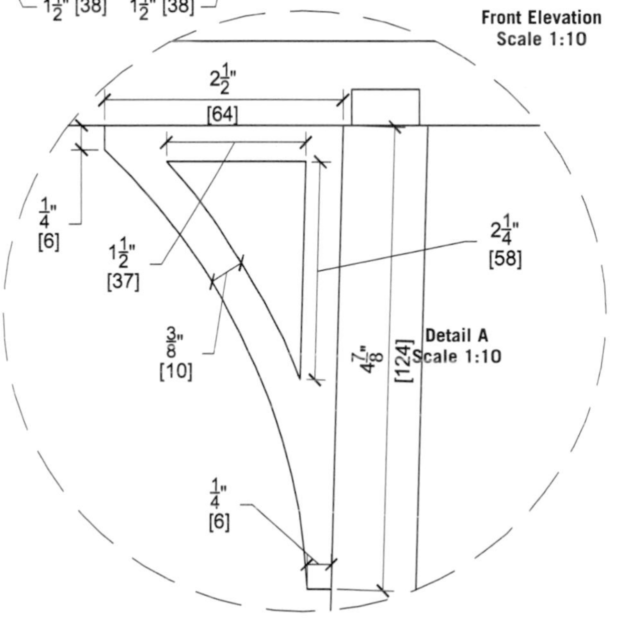
2 1/2"
[64]
1/4"
[6]
1 1/2"
[37]
2 1/4"
[58]
3/8"
[10]
4 7/8"
[124]
Detail A
Scale 1:10
1/4"
[6]

SEE PAGE 6 FOR NOTES ON USING PLANS

CHEST OF DRAWERS IN PALE ASH

A whiter shade of pale

This graduated chest of drawers in the palest, blond ash was made as part of an elegant bedroom set.

One of a pair – this is the 4ft (1211mm) version.

A long-standing client approached me for a set of bedroom furniture – a pair of chests of drawers, one 3ft (915mm) long, another 4ft (1211mm) long, and a matching pair of side tables. The following pages will explain how the chests of drawers were made, the side tables feature on page 66.

Routing out waste from between the pins saves time and makes dovetailing more affordable.

DESIGN

My client had clear ideas about what he wanted and sent me some drawings with overall measurements. He particularly wanted mouldings on the fronts of the drawers similar to some I had made on a previous commission. He also wanted turned columns on the carcass corners, and the whole chest lifted on turned feet.

The columns would have one quadrant removed to let in the corner of the solid wood carcass and the top and base would overhang them, so they would appear completely round from all available viewing angles. The feet under the base would be complete and continue the line. The drawer depths were to increase by 1in (25mm) at each level, and the client chose antiqued brass drop handles.

TIMBER CHOICE

The previous pieces I had made for this client had been in English oak (*Quercus robur*) to match the exposed, sand-blasted oak in his barn conversion home. This time he wanted another solid hardwood, in keeping, but a bit different, and I recommended American ash (*Fraxinus spp.*).

As the drawers were for clothes storage he particularly wanted cedar of Lebanon (*Cedrela odorata*), which I already had in stock, for the casings. Its wonderful scent and insect-repellent properties would add that extra something so important in a custom-made piece.

AMERICAN ASH

American ash is similar to English – the sapwood is nearly white with a darker streaked brown and golden heartwood (often called olive or brown ash). It is generally straight-grained with a uniform coarse texture, machines and glues well and can be brought to a good finish. American ash is often separated and sold as white (*Fraxinus americana*) or brown or black ash (*Fraxinus nigra*). In this case I went for the white-blond wood.

I like using American timbers and find them very consistent, readily available and cost-effective. Waste has been removed and long, wide, straight-edged boards come in a range of thicknesses. I was able to get some nicely figured 1in (25mm) and 2in (50mm) thick boards for this job.

TIMBER PREPARATION

Although the timber was sold as kiln-dried, that had been some time ago, so I cut out all the pieces for both chests to length, plus a little for safety, and 'sticked and stacked' them in my warm, dry timber store to condition.

CARCASSES

To make the carcasses, I thicknessed all the lengths for the tops, bases and sides to $^7/_8$in (22mm), and made each piece up from two widths of board, carefully matched to mask the join. I dressed the edges on the planer and finished them by hand-plane to remove the ripples and slightly hollow the centre of the join. This pulled the ends up tight and allowed for extra drying out and shrinkage.

A biscuit was fitted at each end and middle of each join. This located and held the two boards during clamping and strengthened the join. The biscuits 'grabbed' quickly and held the join while it set, allowing the clamps to be removed early. If you don't believe me, try to take one apart after about ten minutes!

Once all these 'flats' were cured, I scraped the glue-ooze off and belt-sanded them down to 120grit on each side. I dimensioned them accurately and left them sticked and stacked.

DRAWER FRAMES

The drawer frames were made up from 2 x $^7/_8$in (50 x 22mm) strips. I used biscuits and glue for the front butt joints, but on the back joints left the biscuits dry with a gap to allow for movement in the carcass sides. The slots were made in the top and bottom rails for the biscuits, which fitted them to the sides. I shouldered the centre rails to fit into stopped housings in the sides.

FIRST STAGE ASSEMBLY

The stopped housings and biscuit slots were cut in the sides and the drawer frames adjusted as necessary to fit. I cut the shoulders on the top and bottom of the sides, where they eventually fitted into the stopped housings in the top and base. I used a router to make $^3/_{16}$in (5mm) housings in the rear inside edges for the MDF back. Titebond was applied to the front and back biscuits and slots, and the front 3in (75mm) and back 2in (50mm) of the housings, with care taken not to bridge the expansion gaps. I then clamped up the sides and drawer frames. I then measured the diagonals back and front, made adjustments and left to set.

Clamping up the column legs.

BACK

The backs were cut from $^3/_{16}$in (5mm) ash-faced MDF, glued into the slots in the sides, pinned and glued to the back rails. Any small adjustments to pull the carcass square were made before pinning the back.

TOP AND BASE

Stopped housings were cut in the top and base, to take the top and bottom edges of the sides, remembering the 1½in (36mm) overhangs to allow for the columns. I also cut stopped 3/16in (5mm) housings to take the top and bottom of the MDF back. Then I dry fitted the top and base and made any adjustments. I radiused the corners to 2in (50mm) and rounded the edges over with a 3/8in radius cutter. Finally, I used an orbital sander to sand the sides, top and base down to 240grit on all faces and on the front edges of the drawer frames. Glue was then applied to the housings in the base and the carcass dropped on. With the base fitted, I turned the carcass over, placed the top on the suitably padded floor, applied glue to the housings and dropped the carcass on again. I clamped it up and left it to set on a flat surface.

QUADRANTS

The tablesaw was set at a suitable height and the quadrant rebates cut out of the columns for the carcass corners. I located the square waste piece at each end against the rip fence. The columns were trimmed to size, glued and clamped to the carcass.

FEET

When the columns had set, I fitted the feet. The turner had been asked to turn a 1 x 1in (25 x 25mm) peg on the ends. To avoid any discrepancy, a hole was drilled in a piece of thick ply with a 1in (25mm) Forstner bit for him to match to. I used ply rather than an offcut of the ash so that there would be no movement to alter the diameter of the hole. With the same bit, I drilled the fixing holes in the base, using a square to line up the drill and get the hole vertical, so that the feet lined up with the columns. Glue was applied, the feet tapped home and the carcass turned over. Alignment was checked and they were left to set.

Fitting the feet.

TURNED COLUMS

Bearing in mind my own turning limitations and that I required eight columns, eight feet and, for the side tables, a further eight legs, all to match, I decided to subcontract the whole lot to a local turner whose work I had checked out. I prepared the ash blanks and drew profiles, marking the relevant diameters. I cut the column blanks 4in (100mm) over-length and made a saw cut 2in (50mm) in from each end, using the radial-arm saw to mark the exact overall length required for the column. I asked the turner to leave the square section waste pieces on the ends – I would trim the waste off later. I was very pleased with the results when I collected the turnings.

DRAWERS

I cut the individual pieces of the drawer carcasses to size and fitted in the usual way, then carefully marked for identification. The fronts were 3/4in (19mm) thick instead of my usual 7/8in (22mm) and the sides cut shorter to allow for the extra 1/4in (6mm) thickness of the mouldings, which would be fitted to the fronts. Holes were drilled for the brass drop handles but the handles were not fitted yet.

A cutting gauge was used to mark the width and length of the dovetails on the relevant pieces. I cut housings in the fronts and sides to take the bases then taped double pairs of sides together, marked the tails with a sharp pencil, cut them out on the bandsaw and cleaned up with a sharp chisel.

Each side was offered up to its front and the pins marked with a scalpel. I took a router with a straight cutter and set it to the correct depth, adjusting the side fence to cut out most of the waste to form the pins. The job was completed with a chisel. I sanded the inside faces of the drawer carcass pieces and assembled and glued up the drawers. The bases were glued into the slots in the fronts and sides and then glued and screwed to the backs. I checked the completed drawers for square and wind and left to set, then fitted into their relevant places in the carcass, without stops.

Drawer sides taped together so that several dovetails are cut at once on the bandsaw.

DRAWER MOULDINGS

The drawer mouldings were formed on the router table, using an ogee cutter. I thicknessed some wide boards of ash and sanded to a finish. I formed the moulding on each edge and ripped them off on the tablesaw. The edges were refinished and the process repeated until the board was down to about 3in (75mm) wide. Now the board was too narrow to make any more mouldings safely so I used the next wide board.

The mouldings were cut to length on the radial-arm saw, set to cut a mitre, and clamped to the drawer fronts using Titebond moulding glue, which grabs quickly, reducing the clamp time. Once set, I sanded them and fitted the drawer stops so that the drawers were inset slightly.

Clamping mouldings to drawer front.

SANDING AND FINISHING

Usually I do as much of the sanding as possible with belt and random orbital sanders on flat pieces before assembly and on the partially completed piece during construction. This removes glue and clamping marks while the surfaces are accessible. Do a final check over with a palm sander and sanding blocks on the visible surfaces to prepare for the finish.

To keep the clean, crisp, pale colour of the ash, I chose my usual – Aquacote water-based acrylic varnish, which has very little 'yellowing' or darkening effect.

The first coat raises the grain, particularly on ash, and needs to be cut back carefully with 320grit. In warm weather it absorbs too quickly on the bare wood, making it difficult to work. You can solve this by diluting the first coat by 10% with clean water.

Apply the varnish with a paint pad. Apply two more coats on top of the first, cutting back between them with a Scotchbrite grey pad to de-nib. Each coat only takes a couple of hours before recoating. Leave the varnish for seven days to cure fully, then apply a wax finish, buffing it to a nice deep sheen. Fit the brass handles through previously drilled holes and trim the fittings flush with the inside face of the drawer front.

A GOOD RESULT

I achieved what my client wanted and he was pleased with the final result. This was the first time I had subcontracted any of my work and I was impressed with the cost-effectiveness of doing so with the turning. Certainly a lesson learned.

Marking mitre cuts on drawer front moulding.

A whiter shade of pale

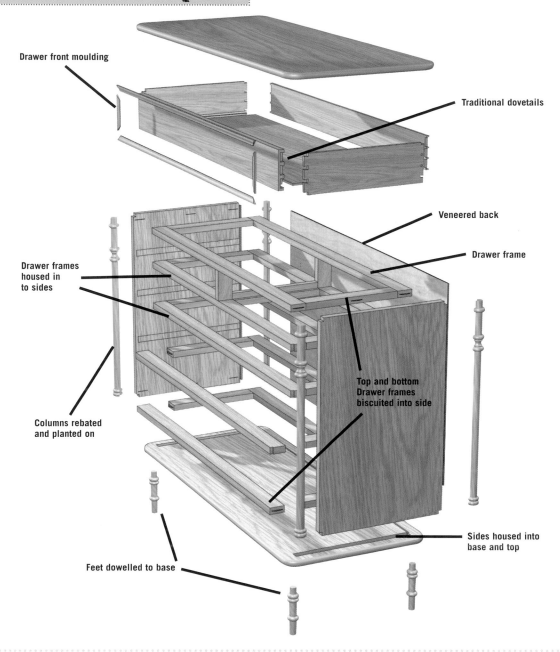

Drawer front moulding

Traditional dovetails

Veneered back

Drawer frame

Drawer frames housed in to sides

Columns rebated and planted on

Top and bottom Drawer frames biscuited into side

Sides housed into base and top

Feet dowelled to base

Another finished chest – the 3ft (915mm) version.

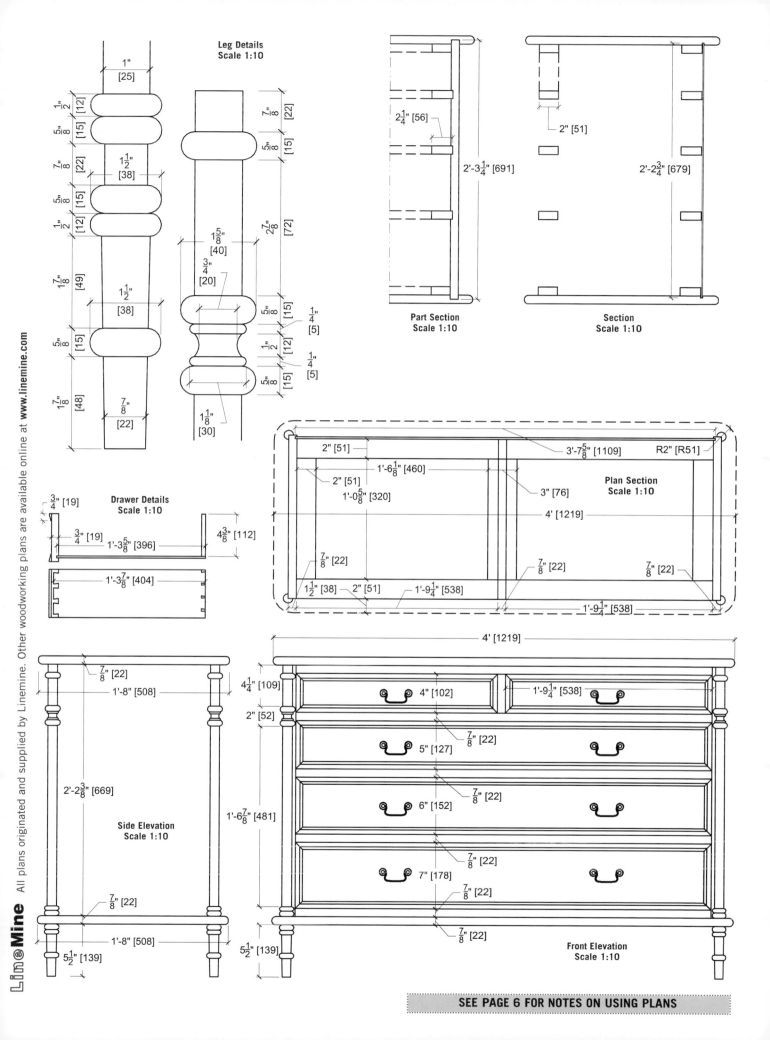

Leg Details
Scale 1:10

1" [25]
½" [12]
⅝" [15]
⅞" [22]
⅝" [15]
1½" [38]
1½" [38]
½" [12]
⅞" [49]
⅝" [15]
⅞" [48]
⅞" [22]
1⅝" [40]
¾" [20]
1½" [38]
⅞" [22]
⅝" [15]
2⅞" [72]
⅝" [15]
¼" [5]
½" [12]
¼" [5]
⅝" [15]
1⅛" [30]

Part Section
Scale 1:10

2¼" [56]
2'-3¼" [691]

Section
Scale 1:10

2" [51]
2'-2¾" [679]

Drawer Details
Scale 1:10

¾" [19]
¾" [19]
1'-3⅝" [396]
4⅜" [112]
1'-3⅞" [404]

Plan Section
Scale 1:10

2" [51]
1'-6⅛" [460]
2" [51]
1'-0⅝" [320]
3'-7⅝" [1109]
R2" [R51]
3" [76]
4' [1219]
⅞" [22]
⅞" [22]
⅞" [22]
1½" [38]
2" [51]
1'-9¼" [538]
1'-9¼" [538]

Side Elevation
Scale 1:10

⅞" [22]
1'-8" [508]
2'-2⅜" [669]
⅞" [22]
1'-8" [508]
5½" [139]

Front Elevation
Scale 1:10

4' [1219]
4¼" [109]
4" [102]
1'-9¼" [538]
2" [52]
⅞" [22]
5" [127]
⅞" [22]
6" [152]
1'-6⅞" [481]
⅞" [22]
7" [178]
⅞" [22]
⅞" [22]
5½" [139]

SEE PAGE 6 FOR NOTES ON USING PLANS

BEDSIDE TABLES IN PALE ASH

Table Talk

Completing the pale ash bedroom set is a fine pair of side tables.

A companion to the chest of drawers on page 60, these were also made as a pair.

These side tables were part of a commissioned bedroom set that included the ash chests described on page 60.

DESIGN

My client supplied design details and overall measurements for these pieces. The design links with the chests of drawers with the turned leg profiles that echo the columns and feet, the shape of the top, the drawer-front mouldings and the brass drop handles.

I left the tops of the legs in square section to simplify the drawer arrangement. The curly brackets under the sides and fronts were a client specification – they do brace the legs but are a little fussy for me.

The client wanted to use them as bedside tables, so the height should be about level with the top of the mattress. I fixed the dimensions of the top once he had decided what was to go on them.

TIMBER

I chose American white ash (*Fraxinus americana*) to match the chests and bought it at the same time. I used cedar of Lebanon (*Cedrus libani*) from my existing stock for the drawer casings.

AMERICAN TIMBERS

I use more and more American timbers these days – there is a good range, they are consistent, readily available and cost-effective. All the waste has been removed and long, wide, straight-edged boards come in a range of thicknesses. You can often even select the width and length of each board. I bought some nicely figured 1in and 2in thick boards (25mm and 50mm) for this job, in sizes that gave little waste.

AMERICAN ASH

American ash is often sold as white or brown ash and as with the chests in the previous project, I used white. For a more detailed description of American ash see page 61.

CEDAR OF LEBANON

This softwood is stable and straight-grained in the main with bark pockets and occasional large knots. It comes in long, wide boards with pale sapwood and golden-coloured heartwood, and tends to warp. Its distinctive fragrance repels insects whilst attracting clients! It's good for drawer casings, chest bases and the internal parts of wardrobes.

PREPARATION OF TIMBER

I cut out the pieces of kiln-dried ash and cedar for both side tables slightly over-length, then 'sticked and stacked' it in my heated, dehumidified timber store to condition.

MAKE THE LEGS

I subcontracted out the turning of the legs, along with the columns and feet for the chests of drawers. However, I prepared the blanks and while they were still square I cut the mortices for the sides, back, and front bottom rails. I drew the profiles and marked the diameters for the turner.

FRAME

The backs and front bottom drawer rails were cut to size. Tenons were formed on the ends to fit the mortices in the legs.

Then I cut the top front drawer rails to size, marked the dovetails and cut on the bandsaw. I marked the sockets required in the tops of the front legs from the tails. The bulk of the waste was removed with a straight cutter on the router, and the sockets finished with a sharp bevelled-edged chisel. I drilled countersunk holes to take the screws to fix the top in the top rail.

All these joints were dry fitted to check accuracy. It was particularly important that they were a good fit, with the joints as strong as possible, as there would be no bottom rails to brace the legs.

ASSEMBLY

All the individual pieces were finished as far as possible with the belt and random orbital sanders, down to 150grit. Then I glued and clamped the front drawer rails and backs to the relevant legs, checked everything was square and left to set, thus forming the table under-frames fronts and backs.

BRACKETS

I cut out all the brackets, glued and biscuit-jointed the front brackets in position. Then cut out the side brackets, finished and glued to the sides with biscuits. I tenoned the sides to fit the legs and cut tenons, on the sides, extending through the ends of the brackets.

Glue was applied to the tenons on the sides, complete with brackets, as well as the mortices in the legs, then clamped in position. They were checked for square and left to set on a flat surface.

Drawer guides, runners and kickers were fitted inside the frames at the top and bottom of the sides. I cut slots in the kickers for the screws to attach the top.

TOP

The tops were each made from two matched pieces, joined with a biscuit-reinforced joint. The corners were radiused to 2in (50mm) and the edges rounded over with a $\frac{3}{8}$in radius cutter on the router, to match the tops on the chests of drawers. I finished to 150grit with belt and orbital sander.

FIXING THE TOP

Expansion brackets were fitted to the inside face of the backs of the frames, with the slots uppermost, set $\frac{1}{16}$in (1.5mm) lower than the top edge of the backs to pull the top down onto the back and legs, when screwed up.

I fixed the front top by gluing and screwing to the front top drawer rail – at the sides with screws through the expansion slots in the drawer kickers, and at the backs with screws though the slot in the expansion brackets.

Drawer sides were taped together to allow multiple cutting on the bandsaw.

DRAWERS

The components of the drawer carcasses were trimmed to size and fitted in the usual way, then marked clearly. The top edge of the backs should be ½in (12mm) lower than the tops of the sides, to ensure clearance for the expansion brackets.

The fronts were ¾in (19mm) thick instead of my usual ⅞in (22mm) and the sides cut shorter to allow for the extra ¼in (6mm) thickness of the mouldings to be fitted to the fronts. I drilled the holes for the brass drop handles in the fronts.

I marked the width and length of the dovetails using a cutting gauge. Housings were made in the fronts and sides to take the bases. The sides were taped together, and the tails marked with a sharp pencil. I cut them out together on the bandsaw, then cleaned up with a sharp chisel.

The pins were marked with a scalpel with each side offered up to its front. I set a router with a straight cutter to the right depth and adjusted the side fence to cut out the majority of the waste to form the pins, final adjustments were made with a chisel. The inside faces sanded, then I assembled the drawer and glued it up. The bases were fixed into the front and side slots with glue and glued and screwed to the backs. I made sure that the drawers were square and not in wind and left to set. Then they were fitted into the carcass, but without stops.

DRAWER MOULDINGS

Using an ogee cutter, I formed the drawer mouldings on the router table. Some wide boards of ash were thicknessed and the faces and edges sanded to a finish. Some shallow passes were made to form the moulding on each edge, then the moulded edge ripped off on the tablesaw to the correct thickness. I refinished the cut edges, making more mouldings until the board was too narrow – 3in (75mm) wide. In order to make any more mouldings safely, I had to use the next wide board.

On the radial-arm saw, the mouldings were trimmed to the right length with a mitre cut then clamped to the drawer fronts using moulding glue, which grabs rapidly, reducing clamp time. Once they were set, I sanded them and fitted the drawer stops so that the drawers were inset slightly.

Using a scalpel to mark a precise knife line while fitting the drawer front mouldings.

Once marked out, waste was routed out between the pins.

Sockets carefully pared to final fit by hand.

SANDING

It is advisable to do as much sanding as you can with belt and random orbital sanders before assembly and during construction, on individual pieces. Clamping marks and glue were removed while the surfaces were more easily accessible. I had a final check over with a palm sander and sanding blocks on the visible surfaces to prepare for finishing.

FINISH

I used water-based acrylic varnish to keep the pale colour of the ash. The first coat raised the grain, and therefore needed to be cut back carefully with 320 grit. Bare wood absorbs too quickly in warm weather, making it difficult to work, so I diluted the first coat by 10% with clean water. The varnish was applied with a paint pad. Then two more coats were applied on top of the first, cutting back between them with a Scotchbrite grey pad to de-nib. Each coat took a couple of hours to cure before recoating. I left the varnish to cure fully for seven days then applied a wax finish and buffed to a nice deep sheen. The brass drop handles were fitted through the previously drilled holes and the fittings trimmed flush with the inside face of the drawer front.

These tables completed the bedroom set and complement the pale ash chests nicely (see page 60). The whole project was a good example of the client having a pretty clear idea of what he wanted and us developing it together. Everyone was pleased with the end result.

Drawer front moulding fitted and cramped in place.

Finished drawer with applied moulding.

Table Talk

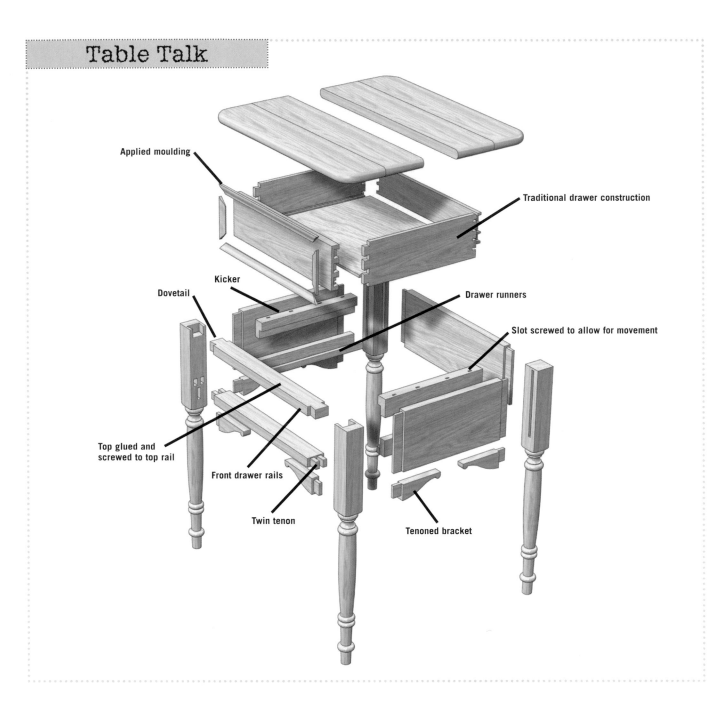

Applied moulding

Traditional drawer construction

Kicker

Dovetail

Drawer runners

Slot screwed to allow for movement

Top glued and screwed to top rail

Front drawer rails

Twin tenon

Tenoned bracket

The completed pair of tables.

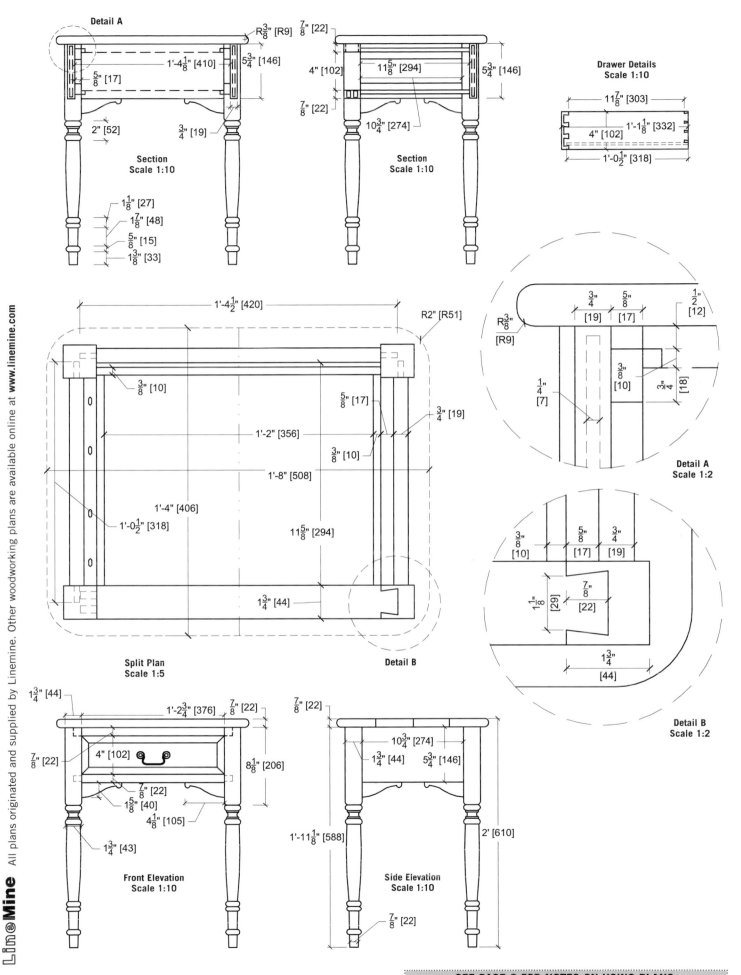

Detail A

R$\frac{3}{8}$" [R9]

$\frac{7}{8}$" [22]

1'-4$\frac{1}{8}$" [410]

5$\frac{3}{4}$" [146]

$\frac{5}{8}$" [17]

2" [52]

$\frac{3}{4}$" [19]

Section
Scale 1:10

1$\frac{1}{8}$" [27]

1$\frac{7}{8}$" [48]

$\frac{5}{8}$" [15]

1$\frac{3}{8}$" [33]

4" [102]

11$\frac{5}{8}$" [294]

5$\frac{3}{4}$" [146]

$\frac{7}{8}$" [22]

10$\frac{3}{4}$" [274]

Section
Scale 1:10

Drawer Details
Scale 1:10

11$\frac{7}{8}$" [303]

1'-1$\frac{1}{8}$" [332]

4" [102]

1'-0$\frac{1}{2}$" [318]

1'-4$\frac{1}{2}$" [420]

R2" [R51]

$\frac{3}{8}$" [10]

$\frac{5}{8}$" [17]

$\frac{3}{4}$" [19]

1'-2" [356]

$\frac{3}{8}$" [10]

1'-8" [508]

1'-4" [406]

1'-0$\frac{1}{2}$" [318]

11$\frac{5}{8}$" [294]

1$\frac{3}{4}$" [44]

Split Plan
Scale 1:5

Detail B

R$\frac{3}{8}$" [R9]

$\frac{3}{4}$" [19]

$\frac{5}{8}$" [17]

$\frac{1}{2}$" [12]

$\frac{3}{8}$" [10]

$\frac{3}{4}$" [18]

$\frac{1}{4}$" [7]

Detail A
Scale 1:2

$\frac{3}{8}$" [10]

$\frac{5}{8}$" [17]

$\frac{3}{4}$" [19]

1$\frac{1}{8}$" [29]

$\frac{7}{8}$" [22]

1$\frac{3}{4}$" [44]

Detail B
Scale 1:2

1$\frac{3}{4}$" [44]

1'-2$\frac{3}{4}$" [376]

$\frac{7}{8}$" [22]

$\frac{7}{8}$" [22]

4" [102]

8$\frac{1}{8}$" [206]

$\frac{7}{8}$" [22]

1$\frac{5}{8}$" [40]

4$\frac{1}{8}$" [105]

1$\frac{3}{4}$" [43]

Front Elevation
Scale 1:10

$\frac{7}{8}$" [22]

10$\frac{3}{4}$" [274]

1$\frac{3}{4}$" [44]

5$\frac{3}{4}$" [146]

1'-11$\frac{1}{8}$" [588]

2' [610]

$\frac{7}{8}$" [22]

Side Elevation
Scale 1:10

SEE PAGE 6 FOR NOTES ON USING PLANS

Settle on Oak

This settle is perfect for storing dusty workshop clothes to keep them away from the 'going out' togs.

The finished piece with the lid open, showing the bearers, to keep it flat.

My clothes fall into the categories of 'going out', 'house' and 'workshop'. The 'workshop' clothes normally still contain a fair amount of dust, despite diligent and energetic performances of the woodworkers' pre-entry dance, with its ritual stamping, patting and brushing, between the workshop and the house. The dust was getting on to the other clothes and there was a danger all of them being downgraded to 'workshop'. The best solution to this problem was to construct some separate storage for the offending items.

Chopping out the square decorative inserts on the arms.

DESIGN

There was plenty of room at the foot of the bed for a blanket box, but I have already made several of those in the past and I like to experiment a little. We decided to add a back, softly curved, tapering arms and leg posts. The under-edges of the bottom rails of the frame were also curved and I added square inserts, reminiscent of through tenons, to the arms to cover the heads of the screws. It had been transformed into a settle.

The bedroom is furnished with an ash bed, side tables, wardrobe, a sycamore dressing table and chair, a sycamore and fumed-oak chest of drawers and the floor is pine. I had elm and burr, mahogany, or oak in stock. We decided to use a light wood, so oak *(Quercus robur)* was voted in.

I had some English 'character' oak left over from a military chest I had made. This was quite pale, with some nice figure, a few knots and some sapwood. Because of the faults and sapwood the oak had been relatively cheap and I had bought a lot more than I needed in case of faults, but was pleasantly surprised with the quality – so I had a well-conditioned surplus. The colour and figure made it similar to the ash at first glance – just a bit warmer in tone. I have sometimes heard ash described as 'poor man's oak'.

THE DEVELOPMENT OF THE DESIGN USING A CAD PROGRAMME

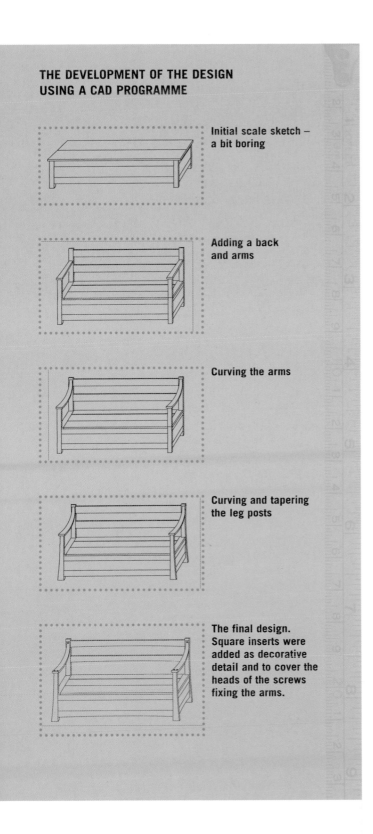

Initial scale sketch – a bit boring

Adding a back and arms

Curving the arms

Curving and tapering the leg posts

The final design. Square inserts were added as decorative detail and to cover the heads of the screws fixing the arms.

CONSTRUCTION

This design is a classic case for the 'keeping it simple' method of construction. Biscuit joints were used throughout, doubled up where possible and appropriate. The only complication in this piece was the laminated arms.

POSTS AND RAILS

The leg posts and rails for the sides, front and back were cut to their full size and double biscuit slots were made. I set the back face of the front and back rails flush with the back face of the leg posts, so that the front faces of the rails were inset by $\frac{1}{8}$in (3mm).

A $\frac{3}{8}$in x $\frac{3}{8}$in (9 x 9mm) slot was cut in the centre of the inside edges of the relevant back, front and side rails, to take the panels. I dry assembled the sides and the position of the slot for the panels in the leg posts was marked then cut. A $\frac{1}{4}$in (6mm) slot was cut in the inside face of the bottom front, back and side rails to take the oak-faced MDF base.

The posts and rails were dry assembled and I marked the position of the critical points of the curves on the outside edges of the posts with a pencil. Using a pencil guided by a long straight edge, bent against C-clamps, I drew the full curve, cut it on a bandsaw and finished with a spokeshave, scraper and sanding block. I used the first of each pair as a template for the second.

I marked the under-edges of the bottom, front, back and side rails and the top two back rails, cut and finished the curve in a similar way.

Using a $\frac{1}{8}$in (3mm) radius cutter with a guide bearing on the router table, I rounded over the top end, bottom end and outside edges of the back posts, then the bottom end and outside edges of the front posts. Similarly, all four long edges of the two top back rails, then the under, curved edges of the four bottom rails were rounded over. Then I sanded all these components, with belt and random orbital sanders, down to 150grit, then sticked and stacked them and put them to one side.

PANELS

I made the panels by deep cutting, thicknessing and book-matching timber from some of the 1in (25mm) stock. The centre join was reinforced with biscuits, the panels were cut to size, allowing for the extra $\frac{3}{8}$in (9mm) all round to go into the slots in the rails and posts, then sanded down to 150grit using belt and orbital sanders.

ASSEMBLY

With the panels in place (dry fitted) I glued and clamped up the front and back, measuring the diagonals to check for square, and left to cure.

These are plain panels with no fielding and they fitted well into their slots. I recommend lightly waxing the corners in case any glue seeps from the frame corner joint, and fixes them in place. I learned that lesson some years ago, when a door panel on an elm dresser I had made was fixed at all four corners by seepage from the frame joints. It split in the middle when it could not adjust to the humidity in its new home.

Simple, strong and quick, double biscuits were used on all main joints.

BACK TO BASE

When the front and back was set, the slots for the MDF base were continued from the rail through the legs so that it joined the slots in the side rails and saved chopping the corners out of the base. Then I applied glue to the slots and biscuits and fitted the side rails. The side panels should be fitted dry but the base can be glued into its housing to join the front and back together. I ensured all the top edges lined up so that the top frame and lid would drop on without any problems.

TOP FRAME

A three-sided frame was made to fit on the top of the box formed between the legs, so that the lid could be inset between the legs and forward of the back, clearing the arms and going past the vertical when opening.

I made the side pieces first and cut the insets to go round the legs on the bandsaw. Supports for the end of the lid were screwed and glued to the under faces, and the biscuit slots cut to fit to the top of the sides.

With the sides dry fitted in position, I measured and cut the long back piece of the top frame. The double biscuit slots in the ends of the back piece and the sides of the side pieces were cut. Glue was then applied to all slots and biscuits and the frame clamped up. I measured the diagonals to ensure everything was square, and left to set. When it was set, I glued with biscuit reinforcement to the top edges of the box.

LID

The lid was made from two boards, butt jointed edge to edge, and reinforced with biscuits. Edges were passed over the planer to straighten and square them and then carefully hand-planed to remove the planer ripples. I left the centre slightly hollow. This ensured that the ends were pulled up tight when clamped and allowed for a little extra shrinkage through the end grain.

Titebond was applied to the edges, biscuits and slots, and the lid clamped. I checked to ensure there was no wind, and left to set. Once the glue had set, I rounded over the top and bottom of the front edges with the ⅛in (3mm) radius cutter on the router.

Braces were fixed with plugged screws in double countersunk holes across the underside of the lid. Double countersinking allowed for movement of the lid across the grain while the screws hold it flat. The lid was then fitted with a piano hinge.

Cutting the taper on the arms on the bandsaw.

FIXING

The taper on the arms was marked using a bent steel rule, and cut on the bandsaw. The arms were then trimmed to size, finished on an inverted belt sander, and rounded over the sides and front end. I cut a recess in the front of the top of the back leg post to let the top of the arm in.

I located and clamped in position, marked a recess and chiselled into the underside of the front of the arm to accept the top of the front leg post. The arms were glued and screwed in position, the screws countersunk, the hole squared with a chisel, oak inserts glued and tapped home. The screws into the front leg went into end grain, so I put them both in at an angle forming the shape of a dovetail – this is called 'dovetail screwing'. This technique can be used for nails and in both cases is a stronger fixing.

LAMINATING THE ARMS

To laminate the arms I first made the curve by bending a steel rule between the back post and the top of the front post and clamping and taping it into position. The curve was pencilled on to a piece of hardboard held against the steel rule, and the curve cut out on the bandsaw. I held this profile in position between the arms and adjusted as needed.

Some scrap ply was glued together to make a mould or former, to hold the setting arms. I marked the curve on it, through the centre, and cut out carefully on the bandsaw, thus making a matched pair of male and female formers.

I chose two matching pieces of oak ½in (12mm) wider than the wide end of the arm and 3in (75mm) longer than the curve. Setting the bandsaw up carefully I cut each into six strips just under ⅛in (3mm) thick. I checked that the first strip was flexible enough to follow the required curve, and numbered each one so they could be reassembled in sequence and the side grain would match up.

The first six sequential strips were painted with glue and placed in the former, clamped up, and left to set overnight. When the curve was removed from the former the next day it was held in a sash clamp for a couple more days to be on the safe side. The other arm got the same treatment.

Bandsawn laminates for the arms in sequential order.

FINISH

Most of the machine-sanding was done during the making process, so all that was required was a check for glue ooze. I removed excess glue with a sharp chisel and sanded any marks out by hand.

I used a clear satin-finish water-based varnish on this piece. The first coat raised the grain so after two hours I cut it back, removing the raised grain with 240grit. The next coat was cut back with 320grit, the third and last coat applied and left for three days to cure. It was then cut back with a Scotchbrite grey pad and buffed with a soft cloth. I attached self-adhesive felt pads under the legs to avoid scuffing our wooden floor.

I made this piece very quickly and when I placed it in the bedroom it did not upstage the ash bed but blended quite happily. Now all my workshop clothes are safely stored separately.

One of the arms in the plywood former curing. The previously cured arm is held in a spare clamp to stabilize it.

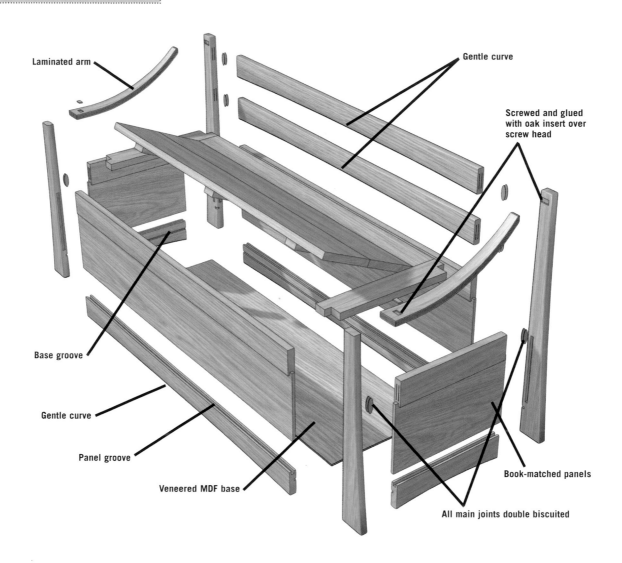

Laminated arm

Gentle curve

Screwed and glued with oak insert over screw head

Base groove

Gentle curve

Panel groove

Veneered MDF base

Book-matched panels

All main joints double biscuited

Visually more interesting than a simple blanket chest and more fun to make too.

Square inserts were added as decorative detail and to cover the heads of the screws fixing the arms.

Side Elevation
Scale 1:10

Section
Scale 1:10

Detail A
Scale 1:2

$\frac{5}{8}$" [16]

6" [152]

$\frac{7}{8}$" [22]

2'-5" [737]

$\frac{7}{8}$" [22]

1'-1" [331]

3" [76]

$\frac{3}{8}$ [9]

$\frac{3}{8}$ [9]

$\frac{7}{8}$ [22]

3" [76]

$6\frac{5}{8}$" [170] $6\frac{5}{8}$" [170]

$11\frac{1}{8}$" [281]

$\frac{7}{8}$" [22]

3" [76]

1'-10" [558]

$7\frac{5}{8}$" [194] $8\frac{3}{8}$" [212]

1'-2$\frac{3}{4}$" [374]

$\frac{3}{8}$ [9] $7\frac{5}{8}$" [194]

Detail A

Detail B
Scale 1:2

$\frac{3}{8}$ [9]

$1\frac{1}{8}$" [27]

$2\frac{1}{2}$ [64]

$\frac{7}{8}$ [22]

3" [76]

$1\frac{1}{2}$" [38]

1" [25]   1'-2" [356]   1" [25]

$2\frac{1}{2}$" [64]

1'-2$\frac{5}{8}$" [371]

$1\frac{1}{2}$" [38]   3'-10" [1168] $1\frac{1}{2}$" [38]

3" [76] $2\frac{1}{2}$" [64]

3" [76]

3" [76] $2\frac{1}{2}$" [64]

$3\frac{1}{8}$" [78]   3" [76]

3" [76]   3'-6$\frac{7}{8}$" [1090] $\frac{7}{8}$" [22]

$\frac{3}{8}$ [10] $\frac{7}{8}$ [22]   3" [76] $\frac{7}{8}$" [22]   3" [76]

$\frac{7}{8}$ [22] $1\frac{3}{4}$" [44] $1\frac{3}{4}$" [45]   3'-10" [1168]   2'-5" [737]

$\frac{3}{8}$ [9] $7\frac{5}{8}$" [194] $8\frac{3}{8}$" [212]

3'-10$\frac{7}{8}$" [1192] $7\frac{5}{8}$" [194]

3" [76] $2\frac{1}{2}$" [64]   Detail B $2\frac{1}{2}$" [64]

Section/Elevation
Scale 1:10

Note: Approx 1 mm gap all round hinged section of seat

$1\frac{1}{2}$" [38]
1" [26]

$2\frac{1}{4}$" [58]

$1\frac{1}{2}$" [38] $1\frac{1}{2}$" [38]

$1\frac{1}{2}$" [38]

3'-7" [1092] $\frac{7}{8}$" [22]

3" [76]

3'-10" [1168]

$7\frac{5}{8}$" [194] $8\frac{3}{8}$" [212]

3'-10$\frac{3}{4}$" [1186]

$2\frac{1}{2}$" [64]

Front Elevation
Scale 1:10

3" [76]   3" [76]

3'-10" [1168]

SEE PAGE 6 FOR NOTES ON USING PLANS

OAK TELEVISION CABINET
The bigger picture

Traditional influences
with simple lines.

**This simple, clean-lined
entertainment centre uses
many modern techniques.**

The back of the cabinet.

Having been trying to convince myself, and others,
for some time that smaller pictures were being
broadcast to my TV, I recently had to admit that the
years had taken their toll and what I actually needed
was a bigger screen. The old TV in its cabinet was
sold and we bought a new 32in flat plasma screen
TV, for which a new cabinet was required.

DESIGN

To fit in with the traditional look of our cottage we
wanted a cabinet to disguise the TV screen and
speakers, DVD reader/writer, the AV connector box
and the digital decoder box. When we received the
installation instructions we found that considerable
clearances were required around the screen for
ventilation purposes. Scale drawings and mock-ups
soon persuaded us that if we included the screen,
the box to hide it in would be too large for the room.

The speakers could be detached from the sides of
the screen to reduce its size and make it relatively
discreet, so I designed a cabinet as a stand to hold
everything inside except the screen, which was to sit
on top. We wanted a simple cabinet with clean lines
to minimize its impact on the room. The speakers
were to be a snug fit inside compartments with a
shelf between them to stack the electronic boxes
and a shelf and drawer under to store magazines,
remotes, DVDs and instruction manuals.

To allow clearance for the drawer, the doors are laid
on the cabinet front rather than inset, and held
closed with concealed rare-earth magnets. No pulls
are needed as the simple feet will lift the cabinet
clear of the floor and allow finger recesses under the
bottom edges. A back is fitted behind the lower shelf
and drawer and on it a four-gang power outlet for the
various components to keep the whole area tidy.

Cut-down backs are fitted at the top and bottom of the speaker compartments for strength and to prevent racking, but leave access to store the rats' nest of spare cable lengths. No back is fitted behind the electronics boxes to allow plenty of ventilation.

Cutting biscuit slots into the side.

TIMBER PREPARATION
The cabinet's materials were chosen to complement our interior. The room has oiled English oak exposed ceiling beams, rafters and floor. We like a mix of timbers in our furniture and French walnut, English walnut, Canadian hard maple, burr elm, elm, mahogany and ash are all present. We decided on through-and-through cut English oak with plain figuring, with an acrylic varnish to keep it light.

I contacted my local timber yard to check there was some suitable oak, and established a convenient time for me to visit and select exactly what I required. When I arrived, armed with a cutting list, chalk and a tape measure, they took me to a stack of oak and left me to get on with it.

I found a nice board for the project with plain figure and minimum waste. I marked the board up from the cutting list into suitable lengths and re-stacked the disturbed timber. We stacked it into the car and I brought it home. Once in my warm, dehumidified workshop, it was sticked and stacked to finally condition before work began.

PREPARATION AND CUTTING OUT
As this piece was for home consumption I decided to use some modern techniques in the construction. This allowed an immediate and long-term evaluation of the technique that I could then pass on. The carcass was butt jointed with biscuit reinforcement, and the doors used biscuits and bead joints instead of mortice and tenons. Biscuit hinges were used, and I made up catches from rare-earth magnets.

All the final trimming cross-cuts of the components were made on my radial-arm saw, so I carefully checked that it was cutting truly vertical through the thickness and at right-angles to the fence. A fair amount of the selection of areas of the board for the various components had been made at the wood yard. I checked over the marked-out pieces, the most important being the door frames and panels as these are the most prominent part of the cabinet; then the top and sides, the remainder being left for the inside components. All pieces were cut slightly oversized, faced, thicknessed and stacked in the workshop.

TOP AND SIDES
The top was from a single piece, cut to exact length and width, the end grain finished with a block plane and the edges rounded over with a ¼in (6mm) radius cutter on the router. On the under face, three biscuit slots were cut for each side and partition using a clamp guide for the biscuit jointer. Housings were cut for the top back pieces of the speaker compartments.

The sides were trimmed to size, three biscuit slots cut into each top edge for the joint to the top, and three on the bottom of the inside face for the joint to the base. Housings were cut on the back, inside top and bottom faces for speaker compartment backs.

PARTITIONS AND BASE
The partitions were trimmed to exact size and three biscuit slots cut in the top and bottom edges for the joints to the top and base. Three more were cut on the inside faces for each of the joints to the shelves. Housings were cut on the back, top and bottom faces for the speaker compartment backs and on the back bottom faces for the back behind the shelf and drawer. After trimming to the exact size, three biscuit slots were cut in the end edges of the base for the joints to the sides. Three more were cut on the inside face for the joints to the partition ends. A housing was cut in the back inner face for the back behind the shelf and drawer.

SHELVES

The upper shelf was trimmed and three biscuit slots cut in each end for the joint to the partitions. A housing was cut in the rear underneath face for the back. The lower shelf was trimmed to fit up to the back, and three biscuit slots cut in each end for the joint to the partitions.

BACKS AND FEET

A top and bottom back for each of the speaker compartments and the back for the shelves and drawer were cut to size from $^5/_{32}$in (4mm) oak-faced MDF. Four feet were cut to size, the edges rounded over with a $^1/_4$in (6mm) radius cutter on the router.

At this point the whole piece was dry assembled to check the fit of all joints. Diagonals were checked and any required adjustments were made.

All the components were belt- and orbital-sanded down to 240grit. I decided to varnish all the components prior to assembly. Accessibility is improved and it is easier to obtain a good finish without dwell marks when the brush or pad can be run off the end of the work without stopping.

We decided on a satin-finish acrylic to maintain the pale colour of the oak so I applied three coats of Aquacote acrylic varnish, hand sanding with 320grit between each coat.

ASSEMBLY

Once the varnish had cured, glue was applied to the biscuit slots on the ends of the shelves, the corresponding slots in the partitions and housings for the MDF back. The partitions and shelves were clamped up, checked for square, then left to cure.

Next the base slots were glued up, base clamped onto the centre section and left to cure. The sides and backs of the speaker compartments were glued and clamped next, followed by the top.

The beadlock joint.

DOORS

The door components were cut to size, and double biscuit slots cut on the bottom inside edges of the stiles and the ends of the bottom rails.

The top rails were too narrow for biscuits so I used the Trend beadlock loose tenon system. This uses a jig to drill multiple overlapping holes forming a mortice in each of the pieces to be joined.

A shaped piece of beadlock tenon dowel was then glued into the mortices. I found this quick and easy to use and the results were completely satisfactory.

The panels were fielded on the router table using a vertical fielding cutter, finished with a cabinet scraper, palm sander, and then by hand. The panels were finished with three coats of Aquaseal before assembly. Housing slots were cut in the door stiles and rails for the panels. The doors were then clamped up, checked for square and left to cure. Then the frames were varnished.

Door construction.

Door clamped up.

Marking drawer back from front.

DRAWER

The drawer is dovetailed front and back with an oak-faced MDF base glued in all around. A cutout is made in the front, which allows opening and closing without a pull.

Cutting tails on the bandsaw.

FITTING THE DOORS

The doors were trimmed to size and clamped into position on the front face of the cabinet. The centres of the hinge positions were marked on the doors and the height of the biscuit jointer set so that the slots were centred between the door stiles and the cabinet front. The hinge depth setting marked on the jointer was set and a slot cut for each hinge – very accurate and much quicker than recessing butt hinges. The holes for the screws were drilled using a self-centring hinge drill. This is a very useful, cheap drill and guide to ensure the screw is dead centre every time.

Marking pins from tails.

RARE-EARTH CATCHES

Once the doors were fitted, slots were cut in the bottom of the centre stiles and corresponding slots in the centre of the cabinet base and small rare-earth magnets glued in with Araldite – make sure that the attracting poles are facing each other! The magnets work through about a total of $5/32$in (4mm) of wood – half on each face.

Tapping the dovetails home.

FINAL FINISH

Marks and blemishes were hand-sanded down with a 320grit sanding block and a final thin coat of Aquacote applied to the outside. We achieved the look we were after with this piece, and the use of modern techniques speeded the making up no end. I learned some new techniques and was very satisfied with the result.

The underside showing rare-earth magnet catches and finger recesses.

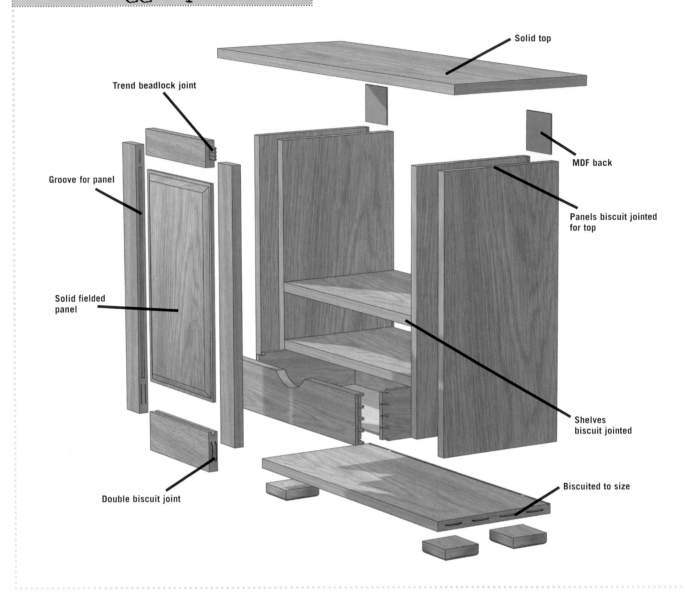

Solid top

Trend beadlock joint

Groove for panel

Solid fielded panel

Double biscuit joint

MDF back

Panels biscuit jointed for top

Shelves biscuit jointed

Biscuited to size

The new TV on the cabinet.

Fitted biscuit hinge.

2'-8$\frac{1}{2}$" [825]

2" [51]

3$\frac{1}{4}$" [83]

1'-4$\frac{1}{4}$" [413]

9$\frac{1}{2}$" [241]

1'-3$\frac{3}{4}$" [400]

1'-1" [330]

1'-8$\frac{3}{4}$" [527]

9" [228]

2" [51]

2" [51]

3" [76]

7$\frac{7}{8}$" [22]

7$\frac{7}{8}$" [22]

Front Elevation
Scale 1:10

11$\frac{1}{2}$" [292]

10$\frac{1}{8}$" [257]

$\frac{3}{4}$" [19]

1'-10$\frac{1}{2}$" [571]

3" [76]

Side Elevation
Scale 1:10

Section
Scale 1:10

1'-4$\frac{1}{4}$" [413]

10$\frac{1}{8}$" [257]

$\frac{1}{2}$" [13]

9$\frac{7}{8}$" [251]

8$\frac{3}{4}$" [222]

8$\frac{1}{2}$" [216]

$\frac{3}{4}$" [19]

$\frac{3}{8}$" [10]

Plan Section
Scale 1:10

10$\frac{1}{8}$" [257]

9$\frac{1}{2}$" [241]

9" [228]

2" [51]

1'-1" [330]

1'-5$\frac{3}{4}$" [451]

$\frac{3}{8}$" [10]

$\frac{3}{8}$" [10]

8$\frac{7}{8}$" [225]

1'-4$\frac{3}{4}$" [425]

8$\frac{1}{4}$" [210]

1'-5$\frac{1}{8}$" [433]

$\frac{3}{4}$" [19]

10$\frac{1}{8}$" [257]

Plan Section
Scale 1:10

9$\frac{3}{8}$" [238]

9$\frac{1}{8}$" [232]

Drawer Details
Scale 1:10

3" [76]

2$\frac{7}{8}$" [73]

11" [279]

1'-8" [508]

$\frac{3}{4}$" [19]

$\frac{3}{4}$" [19]

1'-5$\frac{1}{2}$" [444]

$\frac{3}{4}$" [19]

$\frac{3}{4}$" [19]

2$\frac{3}{4}$" [70]

2$\frac{3}{4}$" [70]

$\frac{3}{4}$" [19]

3$\frac{3}{4}$" [95]

4" [102]

$\frac{3}{4}$" [19]

3" [76]

3$\frac{3}{4}$" [95]

1" [25]

2$\frac{7}{8}$" [73]

$\frac{3}{4}$" [19]

Section
Scale 1:5

2'-0$\frac{1}{2}$" [622]

SEE PAGE 6 FOR NOTES ON USING PLANS

Welcome reception

The company logo was a pivotal part in the design.

Image sells – so when a client started up his third company, I designed and made him a reception desk with panache.

This desk was made for a regular client who had already had two pairs of desks for his various homes and businesses. He had started another company and wanted me to make a less traditional desk for the receptionist of this new cutting-edge operation.

Sycamore gave a clean modern look that suited the company profile.

DESIGN STAGE

We were discussing the project in my study at my own desk, which is of fumed oak, with sycamore door panels and drawer fronts. My client liked the combination of timbers but wanted a lighter overall effect. We arrived at this sycamore desk, with fumed oak door panels, pulls and a plinth, to add drama. He also wanted to incorporate a marquetry version of the company logo.

The lady who was to use the desk was able to try the existing desks at his other company premises and she confirmed the same top size was required.

This would be too wide for drawers or cupboards from one side only so we used the same configuration of drawers at the back, and cupboards in the front as on the previous desks. She chose the version with the shallow cupboard at the front which gave more storage, and would double as a 'modesty' panel. We finalized the design by locating the company logo on the two large front door panels – this would be 'let in' as a marquetry design.

CHOOSING THE TIMBER

I bought some nice clean, kiln-dried sycamore (*Acer pseudoplatanus*) from a local wood yard. Before purchase, I established that it had been end reared when drying, and checked with a hand plane that the grey staining and stick marks did not penetrate too far. I had some pieces of good, straight-grained French oak (*Quercus spp.*) in stock for the contrasting pieces.

Offices and boardrooms can be some of the most difficult areas for solid wood furniture as they tend to be warmer and drier than even domestic conditions. For this reason I was careful to thoroughly condition the timber in my dehumidified wood store for some weeks and keep the workshop even warmer and drier than usual during the making.

CUTTING IT

The whole cutting list was dimensioned, stacked and sticked in the workshop. All the pieces not being worked on remained in the stack, and components, such as the sides and drawer frames, were stacked in a similar way, after making, to continue conditioning and avoid any distortion.

There were quite a number of items of the same dimensions, so it was essential to take care over sequencing of actions, and use rods, jigs and stops for repeat measurements and actions.

I double-checked that I had the correct number (and sometimes a spare) of each item. All the cuts were made at a particular machine setting at the same time, and I double-checked the measurements of the first one, to avoid multiple mistakes!

Drawers at the working side of the desk.

MATCHING THE TOP

The top was made up from four boards which were edge-matched to disguise the joint, and to get the best figure. I machine-planed the edges and finished them by hand, to take out the planer ripples and leave the join length slightly hollow at the centre. This put slight pressure on the ends and allowed for any extra shrinkage of the end grain. Then I cut a slot, stopped 1in (25mm) short of the ends, for Tanseli wafers to strengthen the join.

SIDES IN PLACE

The frame, stiles and rails were double biscuit jointed with the bottom rail deeper than the top to show the same width above the moulded plinth. I fitted an insert to the inner face to house the back of the drawer frames and shelves. The inside edges of the frame were slotted $\frac{3}{8}$ x $\frac{3}{8}$in (9 x 9mm) to take the panels.

I made the panels from solid wood $\frac{3}{8}$in (9mm) thick, deep sawn from 1in (25mm) boards and edge jointed to full size. The panel faces were finished and the inside edges of the frames. I glued up the frames, checked them for square and left to set.

Then I cut out the stopped housings to take the shelves and drawer frames with a router. To do this, I marked the sides clearly as right- and left-handed, and made all the cuts using the router fence. For those outside the reach of the router fence, I made a fixed fence from ply and batten, located at the top of the side for each of the remaining cuts.

DRAWER FRAMES AND SHELVES

The drawer frames were made up with biscuits at each corner. I glued and pinned a ply lip along the outside edge, to fill the gap between it and the side panel, for the drawers to run against. The shelves were cut and finished at the same time. Frames and shelves were shouldered to fit the stopped housings in the side frames, and the partitions between the cupboard backs and the drawers were cut from $\frac{3}{16}$in (5mm) sycamore-faced MDF.

ASSEMBLE PEDESTALS

All the pieces required for each pedestal were laid out and I check fitted them. They were glued and clamped up, checked for square and left to set. The backs were glued and pinned to the drawer frames and the shelves using hardboard jigs, which hold the pin in place for the hammer.

FUMING PLINTHS AND PANELS

The $\frac{5}{8}$ x $3\frac{7}{8}$in (16 x 98mm) pieces of oak for the plinths had an ogee moulding formed on the top edge with a router, and were cut to suitable lengths.

The panels for the doors were made up by deep sawing the selected oak and match jointing in the centre. I fielded them using a vertical profile cutter on the router table. I completely finished and fumed the plinth pieces and the door panels in an old freezer in my garage! They were left over a weekend for maximum depth of colour and penetration, then removed and left for the fumes to disperse. The door panels were sticked and weighted to keep them perfectly flat for the marquetry.

The finished panel.

An old freezer makes an excellent fuming cabinet.

Making the sycamore veneer inserts.

Cutting out the recesses and letters for the marquetry insert on the overhead router.

LOGO MARQUETRY

During the design phase I had remembered about a firm who specialized in CAD/CAM laser-cut marquetry luckily only a short distance away. We had discussed the project with them and they had prepared samples of the logo which had been approved by my client.

I took the door panels over and watched as they programmed an overhead router to cut the oval recesses. The letters and the concentric fumed-oak oval were left proud in the centre and pre-prepared ovals of sycamore veneer dropped in to complete the logo. It was left under a press overnight and collected the next day.

Keeping the panels dead flat had been very important as the machine was depth cutting to an exact 0.7mm for the veneer inserts. Normally the marquetry would have been power-sanded flat, but I did not want to risk any lightening of the oak or bleeding of the dark fumed-oak dust, into the sycamore veneer. So I did the final, very fine adjustments myself, using a scraper, always cutting from sycamore to oak. The panels were dropped into the door frame recesses and held in place with pinned beading.

Hand-finishing fielded panels with shoulder plane, scraper and hand-sanding block.

PLINTH IN PLACE

Biscuits were used to join a backing rail to the base and screwed between the sides at the front and back. I glued and screwed the plinth to it, and the pedestal sides. The mitres, reinforced with biscuits, were tapped over where necessary, and lightly sanded when dry. A gap was left on the inside faces to take the centre cupboards, with an internal mitred corner at the front. I made up the centre cupboard's front plinth at the same time.

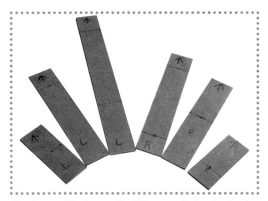
Jigs for positioning and holding panel pins for backs.

CENTRE CUPBOARD

I cut stopped housings for the base and shelf in the centre cupboard sides. Then cut a slot to take the back of $^3/_{16}$in (5mm) MDF faced on each side with sycamore. The base and shelf were cut to size and dry fitted. A plinth backing rail was made for the front. I finished all the pieces, glued, clamped, checked for square, and left to set. The back was glued in all round for strength and the top joined flush down on to the sides using biscuits. I screwed and glued the pre-prepared plinth piece to the front backing rail.

DOORS TO MAKE

The door frames were made first – I dimensioned all the stiles and rails and cut the mortices and tenons. A rebate was cut on the inside edges to take the fielded panels. I finished the inside edges then glued and clamped the frames.

MAKE THE DRAWERS

The drawers were made and fitted in the usual way. The fronts were $^7/_8$in (22mm) sycamore, the carcasses $^3/_8$in (9mm) chestnut and the bases were $^3/_{16}$in (5mm) oak-faced MDF, which was glued in all round for extra strength. For ease of working, I fitted the locks to the fronts of the top drawers before assembly. Bright steel supports $^5/_8$ x $^1/_8$in (16 x 3mm) were fitted to the deep file drawers for suspended files.

SLIDING PAPER REST

The paper rest was made from MDF, flush-faced with sycamore-faced MDF, and edge lipped. Before assembly, I drilled 1in (25mm) holes in the frame under the paper rest, to give access for the screws fixing the top. The paper rest was fitted and a pull attached. Stops were fitted to prevent the rest being pulled too far out.

TRIAL ASSEMBLY

I assembled the desk and made all final tests and adjustments on a level platform on the floor of the workshop. Then the top was attached using screws through countersunk slots in the top rails of the pedestals, to allow for movement. I screwed the centre cupboard through from the inside to the pedestal side frames. The gap was filled between the frame and the panel with a fillet on the back edge of the centre cupboards.

TO THE FINISH

I had sanded all the individual pieces – using a belt and orbital sander – down to 120grit during the making. Once the desk was assembled, it only remained to finally hand-sand to 240grit. To keep the pale creaminess of the sycamore I chose a satin-finish, water-based, acrylic floor varnish. I applied three coats with a paint pad, rubbing down between coats. This is my preferred water-based varnish – it dries quickly and hardens to a tough satin finish.

THE VERDICT

My client arranged for one of his vehicles to collect the component parts of the desk and I went up to his offices one beautiful autumn day to assemble it for him. Once it was in position he was pleased – it was a striking piece – and just what he wanted!

Welcome reception

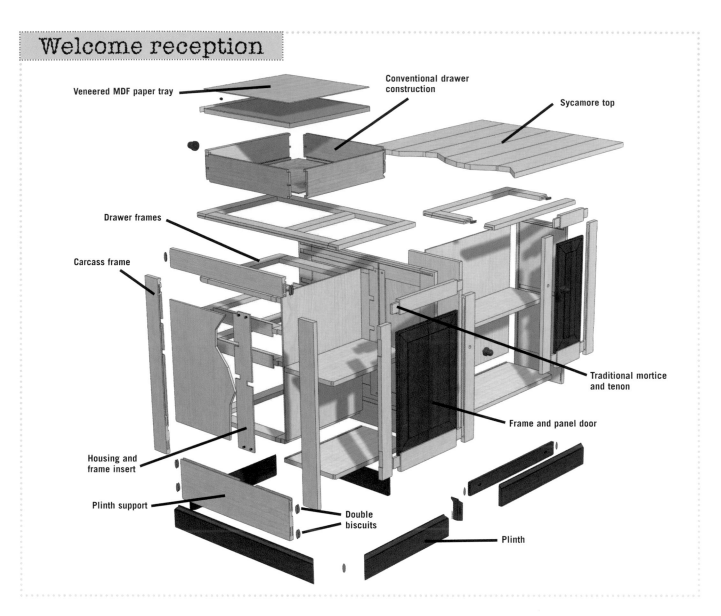

Veneered MDF paper tray

Conventional drawer construction

Sycamore top

Drawer frames

Carcass frame

Traditional mortice and tenon

Frame and panel door

Housing and frame insert

Plinth support

Double biscuits

Plinth

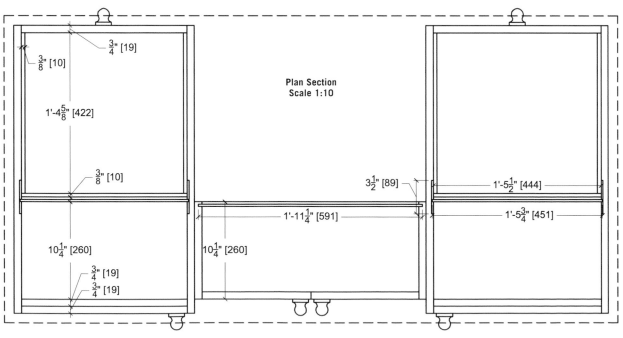

Plan Section
Scale 1:10

$\frac{3}{4}$" [19]

$\frac{3}{8}$" [10]

$\frac{3}{8}$" [10]

1'-4$\frac{5}{8}$" [422]

$\frac{3}{8}$" [10]

$3\frac{1}{2}$" [89]

1'-5$\frac{1}{2}$" [444]

1'-11$\frac{1}{4}$" [591]

1'-5$\frac{3}{4}$" [451]

10$\frac{1}{4}$" [260]

10$\frac{1}{4}$" [260]

$\frac{3}{4}$" [19]

$\frac{3}{4}$" [19]

Side Elevation
Scale 1:10

2'-8" [813]

$\frac{7}{8}$" [22] 3" [76]

2' [610]

1'-7$\frac{1}{4}$" [489]

3" [76]

3" [76]

1'-8" [508]

2'-5$\frac{1}{8}$" [740]

2'-0$\frac{3}{4}$" [629]

3" [75] 6$\frac{7}{8}$" [175]

3$\frac{7}{8}$" [98]

2'-7$\frac{1}{4}$" [794]

Section
Scale 1:10

2" [51] 8$\frac{7}{8}$" [225] 2" [51] 1'-3$\frac{1}{8}$" [384] 2" [51]

$\frac{3}{4}$" [19]

1'-5$\frac{3}{4}$" [451]

$\frac{5}{8}$" [14]

4$\frac{3}{8}$" [111]

2'-0$\frac{1}{8}$" [611]

1'-7$\frac{1}{4}$" [489]

10$\frac{1}{4}$" [260]

2" [51]

$\frac{3}{8}$" [10]

1'-0$\frac{1}{4}$" [311] 1'-4$\frac{3}{4}$" [425]

2" [51]

$\frac{5}{8}$" [16]

2" [51]

Front Elevation
Scale 1:10

1'-4" [406] 9$\frac{3}{4}$" [248] 11$\frac{1}{4}$" [286] 1'-5$\frac{1}{2}$" [444]

2$\frac{1}{4}$" [57]

1'-1$\frac{3}{4}$" [349]

1'-6$\frac{1}{2}$" [470]

1'-7$\frac{1}{4}$" [489]

1'-11$\frac{3}{4}$" [603]

3" [76]

7$\frac{1}{2}$" [192] 6$\frac{3}{4}$" [172]

1'-1" [330]

2$\frac{1}{4}$" [57] 2$\frac{1}{4}$" [57]

1'-8$\frac{1}{4}$" [514] 1'-10$\frac{3}{4}$" [578]

Back Elevation
Scale 1:10

5'-4" [1626]

$\frac{3}{4}$" [19]

$\frac{3}{4}$" [19]

5$\frac{3}{8}$" [136]

$\frac{3}{4}$" [19]

4$\frac{3}{8}$" [111]

$\frac{3}{4}$" [19]

5$\frac{3}{8}$" [137]

$\frac{3}{4}$" [19]

4$\frac{3}{8}$" [111]

$\frac{3}{4}$" [19]

5$\frac{3}{8}$" [137]

$\frac{3}{4}$" [19]

1'-11$\frac{3}{4}$" [603]

5$\frac{3}{8}$" [137]

1' [305]

$\frac{3}{4}$" [19]

1'-5$\frac{1}{2}$" [444]

$\frac{3}{4}$" [19]

$\frac{3}{4}$" [19]

1'-10$\frac{1}{2}$" [572]

1'-5$\frac{1}{2}$" [444]

$\frac{3}{4}$" [19]

5$\frac{3}{8}$" [137]

$\frac{3}{4}$" [19]

3$\frac{7}{8}$" [98]

1'-8$\frac{1}{4}$" [514]

SEE PAGE 6 FOR NOTES ON USING PLANS

BURR ELM APOTHECARY'S CHEST
Good chemistry

This apothecary's chest is great in burr elm but has worked well with different timbers in the past.

The finished piece.

I have made several 9 and 14-drawer versions of this apothecary's chest in different timbers as speculative pieces in the past. They have always been successful and sold well. My wife wanted one for the house and, as I love making drawers, I decided to create yet another version.

BURR ELM

I had the remains of a large butt of burr elm (*Ulmus procera*) in the wood store, from which I hoped to obtain enough suitable timber.

Burr elm has a complex rich figure and colour, offering some stunning patterns and visual effects. However, as with many beautiful things, it also has a downside: wild grain, many live and dead knots of all sizes, in-growing bark, cracks and blemishes. In the same board it can be very hard and quite soft, and humidity can have a marked effect as it absorbs and extracts water relatively easily, causing movement.

It is mainly an isolated hedgerow tree, often not commercially viable to timber merchants, thus frequently ending up as logs. This particular supply was purchased from my log supplier in Yorkshire before I moved to Shropshire.

I had most of it planked at the sawmill on a local estate, only hitting one nail, at a cost of an extra £10 for the lost tooth on the saw blade. After planking, it was air-dried on sticks kept under cover for a year or so and finished as required in my home-made kiln. I left some in slabs for thicker work such as posts and the odd bit of turnery.

I get great satisfaction from using burr elm that would otherwise end up as logs – and it appeals to clients too, which is a good selling point.

DESIGN

The original apothecary's multi-drawer chests were used for storing potions, herbs and remedies. Often all of the drawers were the same size providing a uniform utilitarian look that I do not find visually balanced or pleasing.

In my version, each tier of drawers increases in depth towards the base of the carcass. The drawers are also of different widths on adjoining tiers so that, in good bricklayer's fashion, the joints are crossed.

The carcass showing the inside and drawer stops.

SELECTION OF TIMBER

The burr had been in my dehumidified wood store for nearly ten years and I had been selecting the best pieces out of it as required – it was time for a good sort out. I found some nice burr pieces with some wild-grained, highly figured elm, and a lot of firewood! I also chose some cedar of Lebanon (*Cedras libani*) for the drawer casings.

TIMBER PREPARATION

The final look of any piece is decided with timber selection, never more so than when using burr, and time spent here is seldom wasted. I look for grain flow, figure, faults, colour changes, dead knots etc., cutting generous, oversize pieces of the timber.

Each piece of timber was marked with its provisional end position, aiming for a good flow and visual balance to the chest. As the timber had been stored for some years in my dehumidified wood store, I felt it was ready for immediate facing and thicknessing, though still left oversize in width and length.

Finishing can result in a marked change from the dry colour so to achieve a temporary idea of the likely finished colour treat it with a coat of white spirit.

The final position was then marked on each piece and stacked on sticks in the warm, dry workshop so that conditioning continued evenly during the making. This was particularly important with burr elm and elm – neither are known for their stability! Final dimensioning was as required, just before use.

CONSTRUCTION

I usually like to make a solid carcass for this sort of piece but in this case, the timber was in fairly narrow strips, making for obvious joints in such highly figured stock.

I decided to make a virtue out of necessity and use a frame-and-panel construction for the carcass components. The frames are elm with burr floating panels. The drawer fronts are solid burr enabling small pieces to be used, and the drawer casings in cedar of Lebanon (*Cidrus libani*) for its lovely scent. The drawer frames, runners, kickers, dividers and guides are all from the offcuts or stock.

Tapping a divider home.

Grooving the top for the back panel.

TOP BASE AND SIDES

The stiles and rails for the frames were made from 3 x ¾in (76 x 19mm) strips butt jointed at the corners with double biscuits for reinforcement. A slot was cut for the panels on the inside edge.

The panels were deep sawn from suitable pieces, thicknessed and book-matched. I have found this the most satisfactory way of masking – and even making a virtue of the join in such a highly figured timber.

The panels were belt-sanded, pin knots and small blemishes filled with a proprietary light oak filler coloured to shade with earth pigments as necessary.

The top panel was fielded using an upright fielding cutter on the router table. All were then belt- and orbital-sanded down to 240grit, hand-sanded to 320grit and oiled before assembly into the frame.

This ensured no unfinished timber was exposed if the panel shrunk. As the base panel is not seen once the drawers are in place, it had a fixed elm-faced MDF panel glued into the frame instead of a floating burr panel, thus saving burr and adding strength. The frames were glued up, assembled and clamped.

Once cured, the edges of the top and base were rounded over with a ⅜in (10mm) radius router cutter, and slots cut in the back inside face of all four pieces – stopped in the case of the top and base – to take a ¼in (6mm) ply back. Biscuit slots were cut in the sides to take the drawer frames.

The frames were belt- and orbital-sanded to 150grit and the completed panels sticked and stacked in the workshop.

DRAWER FRAMES

The drawer frames were made from 2 x ¾in (50 x 19mm) strips with the crossrails, that act as the runners and kickers for the drawers, butt jointed to the front and back rails with biscuits.

As there would be little movement in the frame and panel carcass, the back biscuit joint was glued and no movement gap left.

Biscuit slots were cut for the drawer dividers. Half the length of these slots extended into the drawer guides so that the biscuit was not only fixed as the divider but also located the guide.

The frames were sanded down to 150grit, the drawer guides screwed and glued to the crossrails and slightly tapered towards the back, by taking a shaving off with a shoulder plane, to ease drawer running.

Biscuit slots were cut in the ends of the frames to correspond with the slots in the sides, and pockets drilled on the top face of the top frame and the bottom faces of the other frames between the slots, so that screws could be used to reinforce the joints.

DIVIDERS

The drawer dividers were cut to size and biscuit slots cut in the ends. They were cut with two dividers clamped side by side so that half the slot was located in each divider, the open end of the slot to the rear of the divider. This enabled the dividers to be slotted into position, glued and clamped, after the carcass with the drawer rails had been assembled.

On a previous version I had used mortice-and-tenon joints between the dividers and the rails and that meant that the drawer rails, carcass and dividers all had to be assembled and clamped together – too difficult for a simple soldier!

BACK

The back was cut from a sheet of ¼in (6mm) elm-faced MDF. I prefer sheet material backs as they can be glued into the frame and provide great extra strength. In this case, the back was also pinned and glued to the back drawer frame rails.

ASSEMBLY

Glue was applied to the biscuit slots in the frame ends and the carcass sides. Biscuits were inserted into the frame ends that were fitted to the sides and clamped up, checked across the diagonals for square, and left overnight to cure on a flat assembly area. The next day glue was applied to the slots in the dividers that were then pushed into position and clamped.

Taking care to avoid the pocket screws, biscuit slots were cut in the top and bottom edges of the sides, and corresponding slots cut in the relevant faces of the carcass top and base. Glue was applied to the slots, the edges, the top face of the top drawer frame and the bottom face of the bottom frame, then the top and base were clamped into position.

FEET AND PULLS

Blanks for the bun feet and drawer pulls were cut from some lumps of burr and during this cutting a slight, but unusual, noise came from the bandsaw. Checking the waste piece, I found a 9mm bullet, cut neatly in half, embedded in the wood! Fortunately the lead and gilding metal construction of the bullet did no damage to my blade.

The feet and drawer pulls were turned on the lathe as usual, making use of sizing tools to ensure at least the overall diameters were the same. The pulls were of a similar shape to the bun feet – the rounded surfaces showed off the oiled burr nicely.

Fitting a foot – this shows the screw dowel and glued peg.

Using a clamp guide to cut biscuit slots in the sides for the drawer frames.

DRAWERS

The drawer fronts and casings were cut to size. The fronts were made from $^7/_8$in (22mm) burr and the casings from $^3/_8$in (10mm) cedar of Lebanon.

The bases were from cedar of Lebanon-faced MDF glued in all round to add strength. The smell of cedar of Lebanon is wonderful; it repels insects and attracts customers!

The tails were cut out slightly oversize on the bandsaw and finished to size with a paring chisel. The majority of the waste for the pins was removed with a router and again they were finished with a sharp paring chisel.

When trimming the dovetails on the fronts the tools were kept razor sharp and pressure light. The wild grain meant sometimes cutting with the grain and sometimes against, and it would be easy to chip the work. As a last resort, keep the superglue handy.

The drawers were fitted a little looser than usual, and set back about $^3/_{68}$in (1mm) from the front, to minimize any visual effect with the shadow line.

Fitting the drawer fronts prior to dovetailing.

The oil beginning to bring out the colour.

FINISHING

Most of the sanding was done to individual pieces before assembly so I performed a final check over and hand-sanded it all with 320grit to remove any clamping marks.

I chose tung oil for this piece, as I like the deep lustre it gives to the burr and the elm while keeping the surface gloss down.

I applied several coats allowing 24 hours drying time between, ensuring that the oil penetrated deeply and there was no build-up on the surface. After a week or so, the whole piece was buffed up with a soft cloth to a nice gentle sheen.

Good chemistry

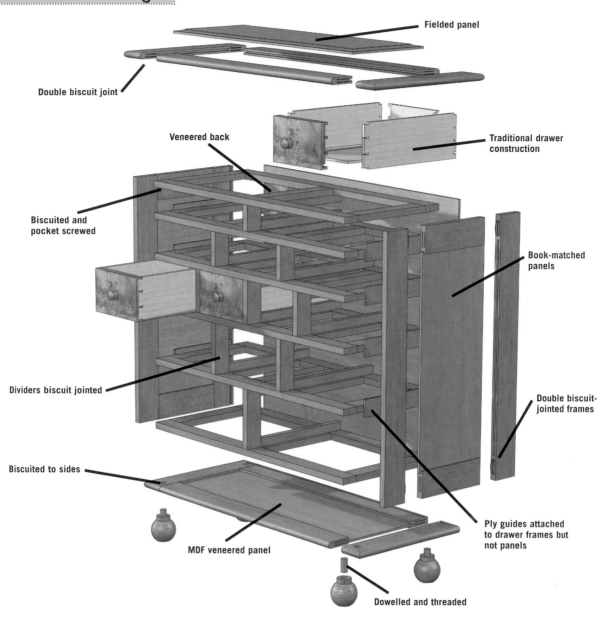

Fielded panel

Double biscuit joint

Veneered back

Traditional drawer construction

Biscuited and pocket screwed

Book-matched panels

Dividers biscuit jointed

Double biscuit-jointed frames

Biscuited to sides

MDF veneered panel

Ply guides attached to drawer frames but not panels

Dowelled and threaded

Elm has wild grain, in-growing bark and many other defects, but its complex rich figure and colour make it all worthwhile.

Some of the drawer components with the dovetails machined, prior to hand-trimming.

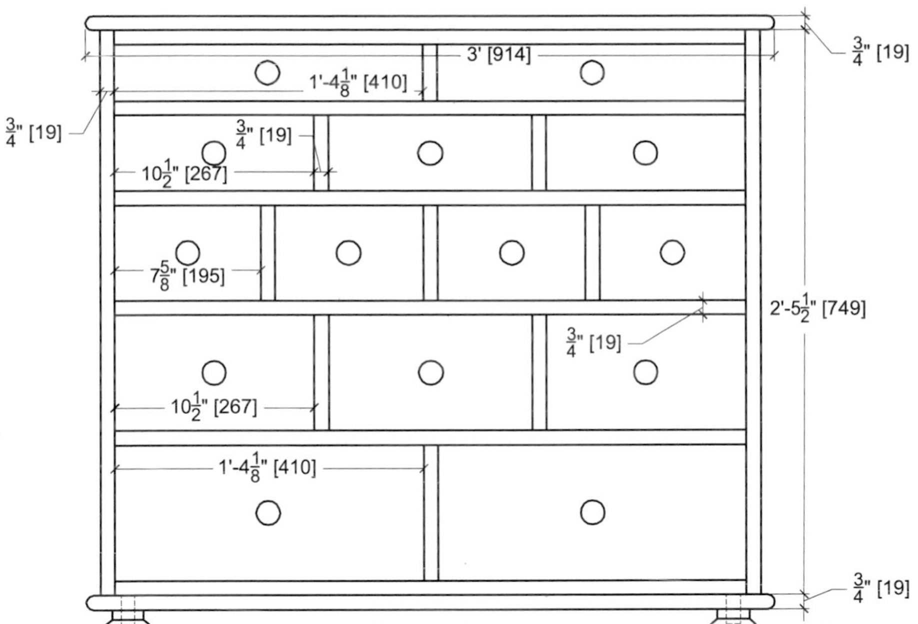

Front Elevation
Scale 1:10

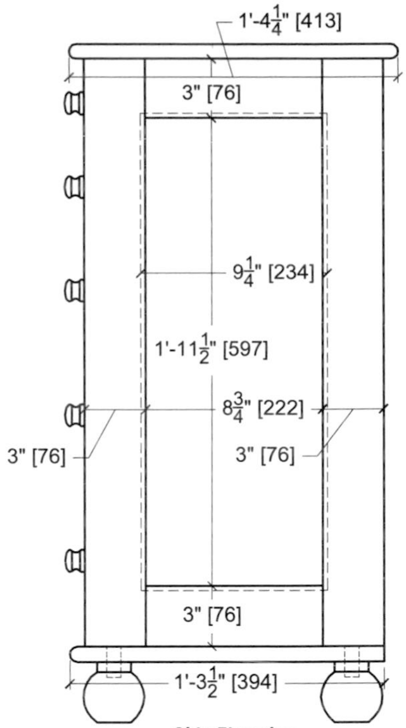

3' [914]
1'-4⅛" [410]
¾" [19]
¾" [19]
¾" [19]
10½" [267]
7⅝" [195]
¾" [19]
10½" [267]
1'-4⅛" [410]
2'-5½" [749]
¾" [19]
3" [76]

Side Elevation
Scale 1:10

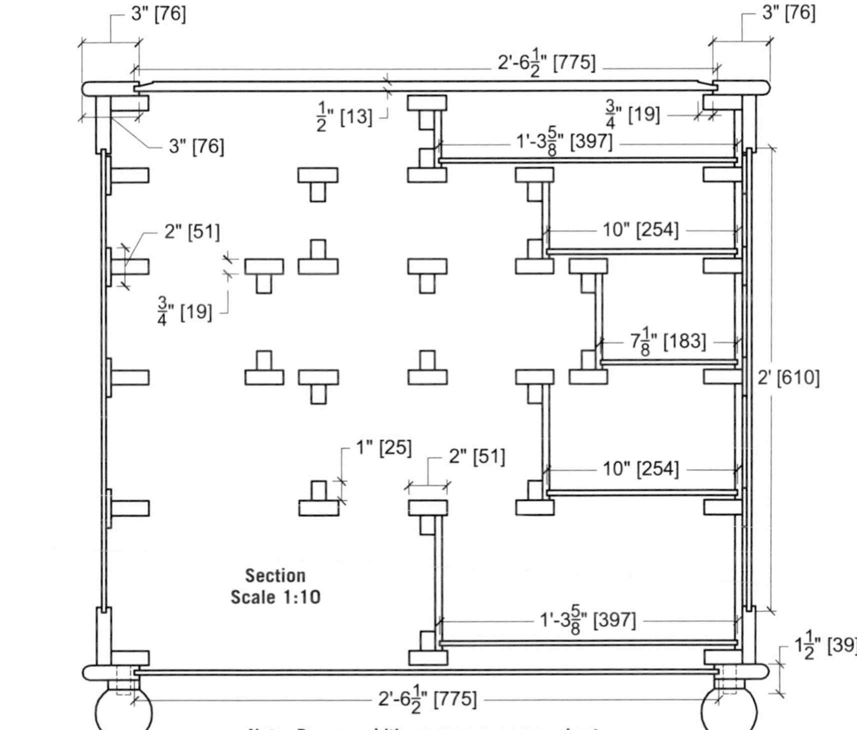

1'-4¼" [413]
3" [76]
9¼" [234]
1'-11½" [597]
8¾" [222]
3" [76]
3" [76]
3" [76]
1'-3½" [394]

Section
Scale 1:10

3" [76]
3" [76]
3" [76]
2'-6½" [775]
½" [13]
¾" [19]
1'-3⅝" [397]
2" [51]
10" [254]
¾" [19]
7⅛" [183]
1" [25]
2" [51]
10" [254]
2' [610]
1'-3⅝" [397]
1½" [39]
2'-6½" [775]
3" [76]

Note: Drawer widths may vary across chest

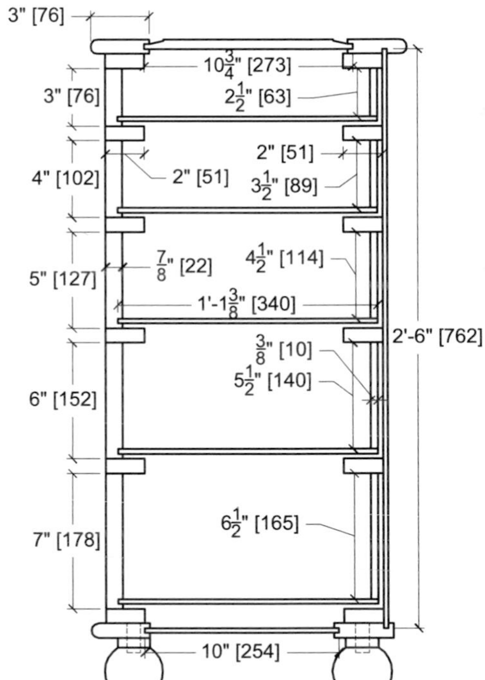

Section
Scale 1:10

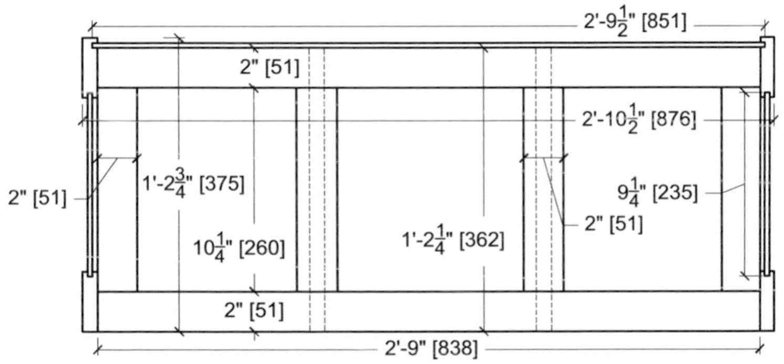

3" [76]
10¾" [273]
2½" [63]
3" [76]
2" [51]
4" [102]
2" [51]
3½" [89]
5" [127]
⅞" [22]
4¼" [114]
1'-1⅜" [340]
⅜" [10]
6" [152]
5½" [140]
2'-6" [762]
7" [178]
6½" [165]
10" [254]

Plan Section
Scale 1:10

2'-9½" [851]
2" [51]
2'-10½" [876]
1'-2¾" [375]
9¼" [235]
2" [51]
2" [51]
10¼" [260]
1'-2¼" [362]
2" [51]
2'-9" [838]

Drawer Details
Scale 1:10

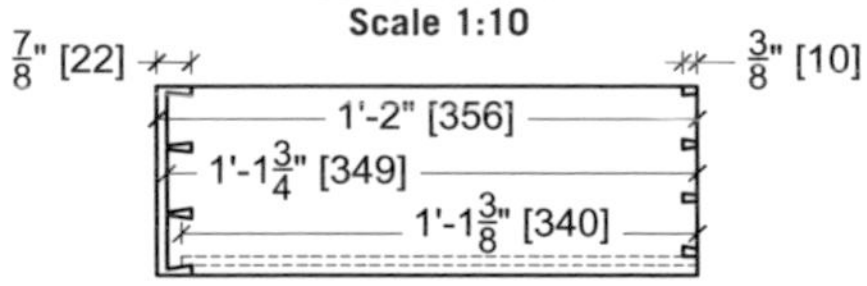

⅞" [22]
⅜" [10]
1'-2" [356]
1'-1¾" [349]
1'-1⅜" [340]

SEE PAGE 6 FOR NOTES ON USING PLANS

Counter measures

An interesting oak counter commission, good timber and a nice friendly client – sometimes life's not so bad after all.

Carefully matched veneers on the front give continuity.

My client for this oak counter project needed a special counter and workstation desk for the shop she was opening. She requested that the counter should have a cash drawer, with a lock, a sliding shelf to hold wrapping tissue paper, be strong enough to wrap goods on, have shelves underneath to hold large and small carrier bags, and a slot to hold clothes hangers on the counter end.

The counter was to be one leg of an L-shaped unit with a workstation desk as the other. The desired look was clean, neat and light. A curve on the outside of one end gave the customer a friendly flow into the shop. Sliding doors on the back kept things visually tidy and saved space, and supported a sliding shelf on filing-drawer runners.

CUTTING OUT

I cut out and prepared the oak straight away, as it would condition better after dimensioning. Intake of moisture is from the outside in, so cutting out and thicknessing would expose the under surfaces, allowing them to dry out. The longest pieces were cut first, the best for the tops and visible faces and the remainder for internal components. All was sticked and stacked and left for some weeks to condition.

UNDER CONSTRUCTION

The top, base, end, shelves and partition were all made up to width by edge jointing the pre-cut, conditioned boards. The edges were straightened on the planer and hand-finished with a jackplane to remove the ripples and leave the centre of the join slightly hollow. This ensured the ends would pull up tightly when clamped. End grain loses moisture faster than the rest of the board, and this pressure helps to reduce the risk of splitting.

Glue ooze was scraped off and the panels were cut to exact size. The curve was marked on the shelf, using a bent steel rule as a pattern, cut on the bandsaw and finished with a plane and belt sander. I used the shelf as a pattern for the base. It was marked out using a spacer between it and the pencil, and the same method was employed to mark out the curve on the top. Both were cut out on the bandsaw, supported on roller stands and finished in the same way as the shelf. The underside of the base was finished with three coats of Aquacote Satin.

TIMBER

My client and I decided on American white oak (*Quercus alba*). It was a particularly good buy at the time as the dollar exchange rate was very good. I like American timbers – they are consistent, high quality and easily available. I went to my local joinery supplier and selected from a batch of 9in x 10ft (230mm x 3050mm) straight-edged planks and, even though I was working on another project, I had it delivered immediately. I like to condition imported timber for a good while in the workshop, which is heated and dehumidified, because one doesn't know how it has been treated, or even how long it has been since it was kiln-dried.

Pressing the front onto the shelves and partition back.

Pocket screwing proved a strong way of clamping a difficult piece.

SIDE

The side was frame and panel construction, as its grain would be in the wrong direction to allow for movement if it were solid. The frame was solid oak with biscuit-jointed corners, and the ply panel was oak-faced on each side, glued in all round to give extra strength.

DRAWER FRAMES

These were made from oak and biscuit jointed. The joints at the front were glued but left dry at the back with an expansion gap to allow for movement in the carcass. Slots were cut in the underside of the bottom frame front rail to take the sliding door track.

POST, FRONT, FEET

An oak post, to frame the join in the ply front and support the back corner of the drawer rails, was cut to size. The two front panels were cut from $^5/_{32}$in (4mm) ply, oak veneered on each face, the grain running vertical to assist the curve.

The feet were turned on the lathe from some 3in (75mm) stock, a 1in (25mm) dowel formed on the ends for fitting to the base, and again finished with three coats of Aquacote Satin.

JOINT PREPARATION

Slots were cut with the router, using its side fence as a guide, in the top, base, front post, end and side to take the front panels. Biscuit slots were then cut for the shelves, partition, drawer frames, central divider and front post. The corners were cut out of the ends of the front drawer rails so they fitted flush with the side. A notch was cut in the front post, as was a corresponding notch in the shelf back edge to form a dry, lapped, bridle joint to support the shelf. Blind 1in (25mm) holes were drilled in the base with a Forstner bit to take the feet dowels.

POCKET SCREWS

This carcass was awkward to clamp with its curved end, so I decided to try pocket screws to pull up and reinforce the biscuit joints, where necessary. I used the Trend pocket jointer jig, as there were quite a few to do, and it could be set accurately for repeats. I tried a few joints in some scrap wood, and was very impressed with the amount of 'pull up', and the strength of the finished joint. The biscuits prevented any slip when driving the screws, and the mechanical hold of the screws allowed work to continue while the glue set. This jig is a very useful addition to my workshop armoury.

Checking for square during dry assembly.

PREPARATION

All joints were dry assembled to check the fit. The components were finished with plane, scraper, a belt sander and a random orbital sander to 150grit. The shelf and partition fronts were rounded over using a radius cutter with guide bearing on the router.

The workshop was cleaned up and tidied and all the relevant tools and fixings were checked and made ready, the glue pot was filled and assembly began.

SEQUENCE

First the end was butted to the base with biscuits and fixed with pocket screws from the underside. Next the small shelf was fitted to the end with biscuits to locate it and pocket screws underneath. The partition was then fitted to the base with biscuits and dovetail screws from underneath, and to the small shelf with more dovetail screws.

The bottom drawer frame was fitted to the end with glued biscuits in the front and back rails drawn up and reinforced with pocket screws. A dry locating biscuit in the centre of the crossrail allowed movement in the expansion gap.

The top drawer rail was fitted in a similar way with the drawer central divider biscuited between the crossrails. The front post was fitted to the base with a locating biscuit and dovetail screwed through from underneath. It was fitted to the drawer rail ends with biscuits and pocket screws in the same way as the other ends were to the side.

The large shelf was now secured to the partition with biscuits and pocket screws, taking care to avoid the screws fitting the small shelf. The notch in the back of the shelf was fitted into the notch in the front post for support.

The frame and panel side was biscuit jointed to the front drawer rail ends and the large shelf front end, with a pocket screw to reinforce it all. The carcass was raised onto blocks and the bottom rail of the side frame edge jointed to the base with biscuit reinforcing, clamped up and left to cure.

FRONT PANELS

The next day I applied glue to the slots in the base, end and front post before gluing the relevant back edges of the shelves, partition and drawer rails. The large, flat, front ply panel was next sprung into the slots, weighted down onto the back edges, clamped to the top rail and left to set.

The smaller curved front panel was lightly misted over with clean water on the outside face and sprung into the relevant dry slots in the carcass to encourage the curve and help with subsequent fitting. Once the first panel had set, the feet were fitted by applying glue to the dowel holes, using a dowel screw in the centre of the dowel to pull them up tight.

Glue was then applied to the slots in the base, front post, side panel and shelf back. The curved panel was sprung into position, strap clamped and wedged to the shelf back and left to set.

The end corners of the top were radiused to 4in (100mm), and the edges were rounded over using a $\frac{3}{8}$in (10mm) radius, bearing-guided router cutter. A cove slot was made in the end for coat hangers. Locating biscuit slots were cut in the top of the end and the side, also corresponding slots in the top.

The top edges of the ply front were rounded over with a sanding block to make it easier to enter into the slot in the top. I applied some glue to the front panel, the biscuit slots, the top drawer front and back rails, fitted the biscuits and dropped the top on. It took a some adjustment, plus a few smart taps with the rubber mallet to get everything into the slots before it could be clamped down.

Clamping the curved panel with a strap clamp.

SLIDING DOORS

The door frames were biscuit jointed and a floating fielded panel fitted. Slots were cut in the bases for the lower guides, and blind $1\frac{3}{8}$in (35mm) holes in the top rails were made to take the running gear. Cove slot finger recesses were cut in the fronts, rather than pulls, to allow the doors to cross without fouling. A guide pin for the lower door guides was drilled into the carcass base. All my door fittings came from Häfele, and the instructions and measurements followed very successfully.

SLIDING SHELF

The shelf was made from a lipped piece of oak-veneered blockboard with support rails glued and screwed under. I fitted filing-drawer runners to bear up to 35kg, again with instructions from Häfele.

CASH DRAWER

This was made up in the usual way, and was dovetailed front and back. A cylinder rim lock was drilled into the inside of the drawer front and the striking plate fitted to the drawer rail above. This is an anti-pilfering, rather than a full security lock.

PULLS

The pulls were my client's choice and worked well in the boutique setting. From scrap, I made a small writing board with felt buttons on the back, to protect the top from ballpoint pens, and I had the pleasure of receiving the first cheque written on it.

Shaping the top.

Adding feet was another way to keep the piece light.

Finishing the inside with lemon oil.

FINISH

The whole piece was checked for glue ooze and marks, which were removed, and was hand-sanded down to 320grit. Three coats of Aquacote satin water-based acrylic varnish were applied to the outside surfaces and cut back between coats with a 320grit sanding block. The final coat was buffed with a Scotchbrite grey pad. The inside was treated with lemon oil, which is a matt sealing and almost invisible, water-resistant finish, with a nice aroma, ideal for the insides of cabinets and drawers.

CONCLUSION

This client was a pleasure to deal with, so friendly and enthusiastic about the whole project and so pleased with the result, even calling me a few days after delivery to say again how good it looked.

Counter measures

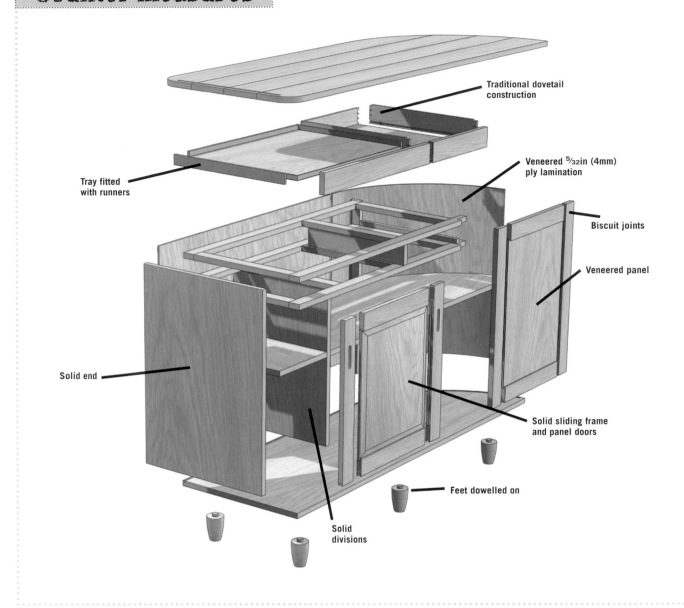

Traditional dovetail construction

Veneered 5/32in (4mm) ply lamination

Biscuit joints

Veneered panel

Tray fitted with runners

Solid end

Solid sliding frame and panel doors

Feet dowelled on

Solid divisions

Behind the scenes – all the necessary practical bits.

Designed to be both light and functional, the curved end gives the counter a softer look.

Section
Scale 1:10

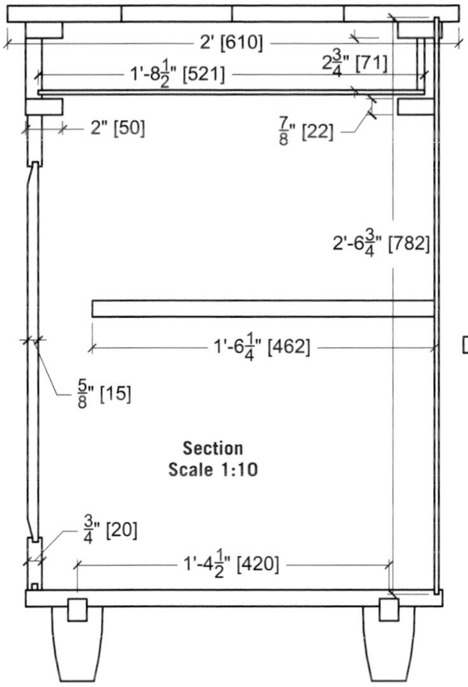

2' [610]
1'-8½" [521]
2¾" [71]
2" [50]
⅞" [22]
2'-6¾" [782]
1'-6¼" [462]
⅝" [15]
¾" [20]
1'-4½" [420]

Part section through drawer
Scale 1:10

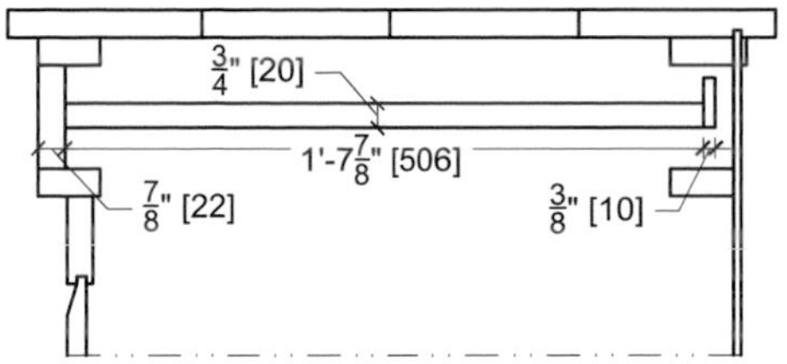

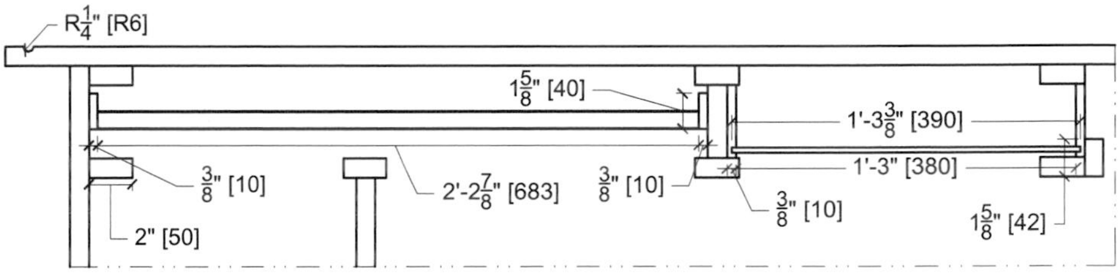

¾" [20]
1'-7⅞" [506]
⅞" [22]
⅜" [10]

Part section through drawers
Scale 1:10

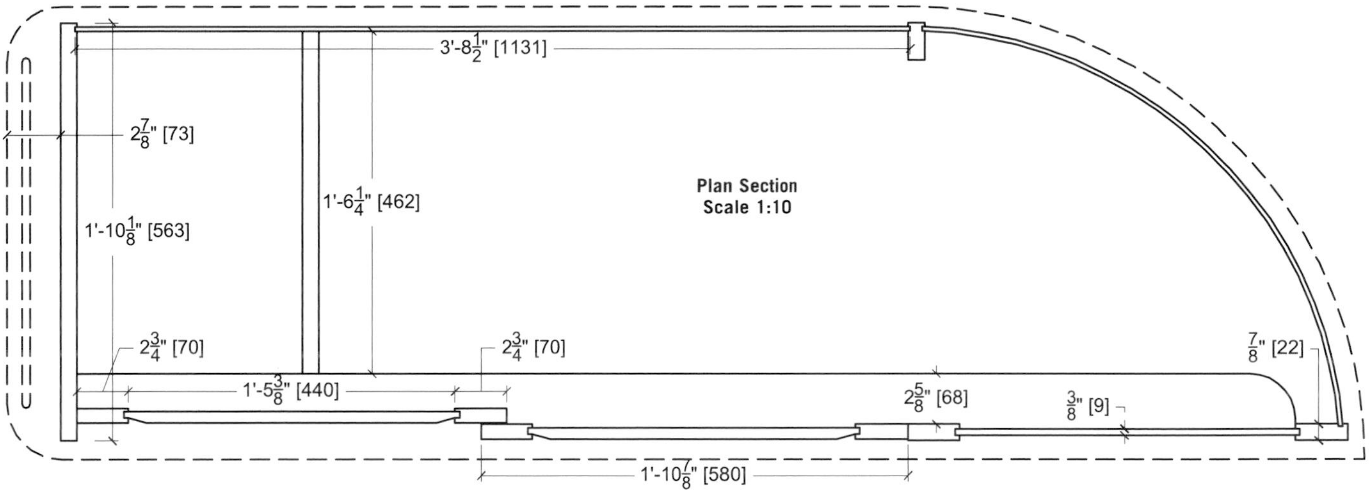

R¼" [R6]
1⅝" [40]
1'-3⅜" [390]
1'-3" [380]
⅜" [10]
2'-2⅞" [683]
⅜" [10]
⅜" [10]
1⅝" [42]
2" [50]

Plan Section
Scale 1:10

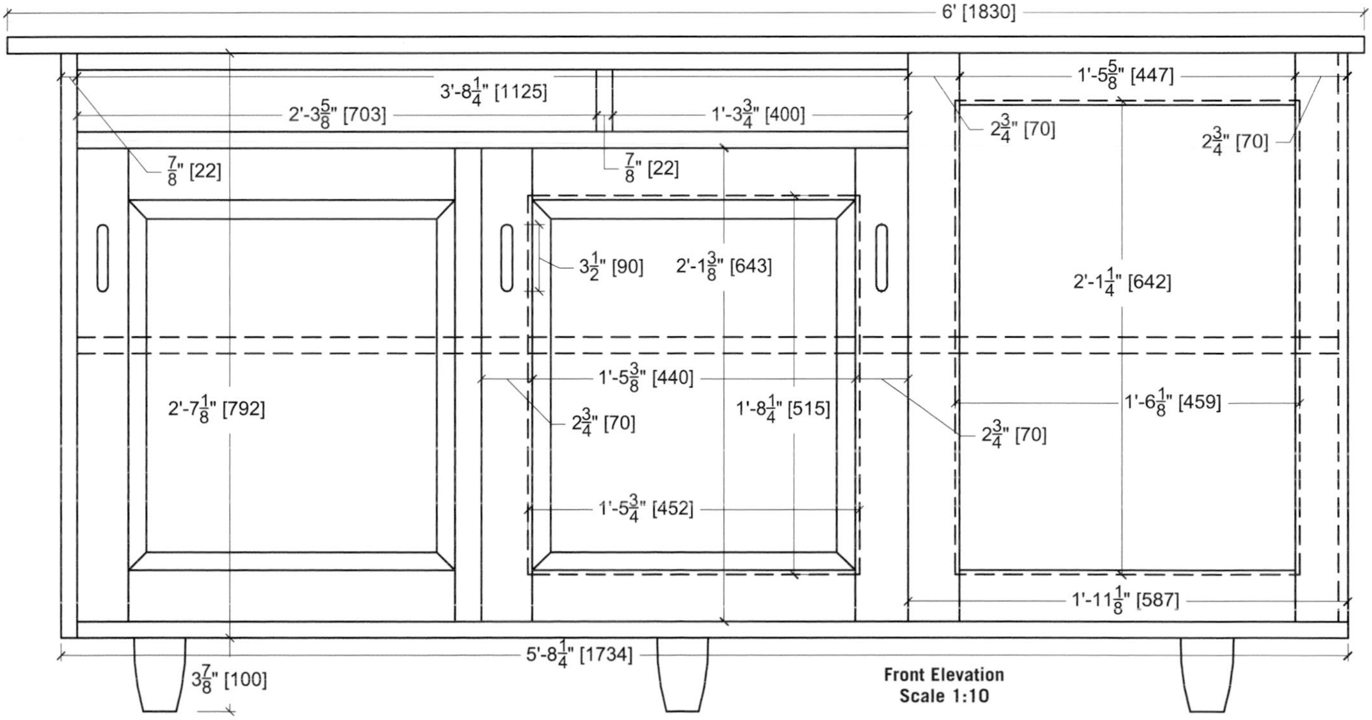

3'-8½" [1131]
2⅞" [73]
1'-6¼" [462]
1'-10⅛" [563]
2¾" [70]
2¾" [70]
⅞" [22]
1'-5⅜" [440]
2⅝" [68]
⅜" [9]
1'-10⅞" [580]

Front Elevation
Scale 1:10

6' [1830]
1'-5⅝" [447]
3'-8¼" [1125]
2'-3⅝" [703]
1'-3¾" [400]
2¾" [70]
2¾" [70]
⅞" [22]
⅞" [22]
3½" [90]
2'-1⅜" [643]
2'-1¼" [642]
1'-5⅜" [440]
2¾" [70]
1'-8¼" [515]
1'-6⅛" [459]
2'-7⅛" [792]
2¾" [70]
1'-5¾" [452]
1'-11⅛" [587]
3⅞" [100]
5'-8¼" [1734]

SEE PAGE 6 FOR NOTES ON USING PLANS

OAK DESK
Up on a pedestal

Following on from the last project is a matching desk to go with the American oak counter.

The client enjoys using her desk, almost as much as I enjoyed making it.

This client was setting up a boutique in a local town, and needed a special counter and workstation desk. Here I will describe the making of the American oak desk, see page 96 for the counter project.

DESIGN

The client quickly decided that light oak with a satin finish would suit the décor of the boutique, and I was able to recommend American oak (*Quercus alba*). The counter and desk were to be complementary, forming an 'L' shape with the counter as one leg and the desk as the other. The main function of the desk was to store documents and records and provide a surface to sit at for paperwork. The back of the desk would be against a glazed wall near the entrance, so the desk would screen the back of the counter. A top unit was required to increase the height, so that the desk could not be easily overlooked through the wall.

A pedestal design was chosen – two simple cupboards with overlaid doors, and a top unit with four drawers fitted to the working surface. As with the counter, short legs were fitted to lift the whole unit off the floor, lightening its look.

JOINTS

As the budget was tight, I kept the joints simple and used biscuits and pocket screws where possible. I used the cheaper American oak, reduced the top drawer unit from eight drawers to four, overlaid rather than inset the doors, and fitted ply backs, oak-faced on both sides, rather than solid wood.

After full discussion, I produced some drawings, specification and my price, which had no slack in it at all. Although it was more than her original budget, she agreed.

TIMBERS

I was pleased that American oak was the chosen timber. American timbers are consistent, high quality and easily available. I went to my local joinery supplier and selected from a batch of 9 x 120in (230 x 3048mm) straight-edged planks and, even though I was working on another project, I had it delivered immediately. I like to condition imported timber for a good while in the workshop, which is heated and dehumidified, because one doesn't know how it has been treated, or even how long it has been since it was kiln-dried.

CUTTING OUT

I cut out and prepared all the oak for the counter and the desk, as it would condition better after dimensioning. Any intake of moisture is from the outside in, so cutting out and thicknessing would expose the under surfaces allowing them to dry out.

The longest pieces were cut first, the best for the tops and visible faces, the remainder for internal components. All was sticked and stacked and left for some weeks in my timber store, which is heated and dehumidified, to condition. The wood was a good light, consistent colour, with some nice soft figure – just what we wanted.

IN CONSTRUCTION

The edges of the three boards for the top were straightened on the planer and the ripples hand-planed out. They were arranged for the best colour and figure match, biscuits were fitted in the edges for reinforcement, glue was applied and clamped up. Once set the top was finally cut to exact size, and the edges rounded over with a radius cutter on the router. It was stored flat for even conditioning.

PEDESTALS

The pedestals were a simple box construction of sides, base and front and back top rails, and the ply back. The wide pieces were made up from narrower boards in the same way as the top and cut to exact dimensions when set. Slots were cut for the ply back, holes drilled for the feet dowels on the pillar drill, and the inside faces and both sides of the back ply panels were belt and random orbital sanded down to 150grit before assembly.

Clamping a pedestal – cross-clamp to pull square.

The top rails and base were attached to the sides with biscuits and pocket screws. The pocket screws were out of sight in the underside of the base and the topside of the rails. The biscuits strengthen the joint and prevent it slipping when the screws are pulled up. The back was glued into the slots, strengthening the construction and helping to prevent racking.

FEET

The feet were turned on the lathe from some 3in (75mm) stock. A 1in (25mm) dowel was then formed on the ends for fitting to the base and the feet finished with three coats of Aquacote Satin. A screw dowel was fitted into the centre of the turned dowel. This pulled up the feet tight into the drilled blind holes in the base when glue was applied to the dowels and they were screwed in. The bases were finished with three coats of Aquacote before the feet were fitted.

Pieces and clamps laid out and prepared for clamping pedestal.

Fitting a foot – turned dowel on foot to blind hole in base with a screw dowel to pull it up tight while the glue sets.

DOORS

Door frame construction using biscuit joints.

We had decided on overlaid doors, which are quicker to fit and give clean lines. The frames were made up, slightly oversize, from 3in (75mm) stiles and rails that were double biscuit jointed at each corner and slotted to take the fielded panels.

The panels were deep sawn from $1\frac{1}{2}$in (36mm) oak and book-matched. The fielding was achieved with an upright cutter on the T9 router fitted to my router table. The fieldings were finished with a cabinet scraper and palm sander, and the panels were sanded and completely finished before fitting into the frames. Once fitted, glue was applied to the biscuits, and slots and the frames were assembled, clamped, checked for square and left to set.

FITTING THE DOORS

Butt hinges were recessed into the doors and the doors fitted onto the pedestal sides. Once fitted, they were trimmed to size and double ball catches fitted top and bottom. The doors were removed and the frames sanded and finished before the pulls, provided by my client, were fitted.

Fitting door hinges.

KNEEHOLE BACK

The inner faces of both pedestal sides were slotted for the ply back to the kneehole recess, as were the top and bottom rails. Biscuit slots and screw pockets were cut in the back faces of the top and bottom rails. The ply back panel was then cut to size and all three pieces finished with three coats of Aquacote.

FINISH

The doors and pedestals were finished before the desk unit was assembled. They were hand-sanded down to 240grit and the outsides were then finished with three coats of Aquacote water-based acrylic varnish. The grain raised by the first coat was sanded down with 240grit, the second coat with 320grit and the last coat with a Scotchbrite grey pad to give a nice satin sheen.

ASSEMBLY

The kneehole back ply panel was glued into the slots in the top and bottom rails then into the slots in the pedestals. The top and bottom rails were fitted to the pedestals with pocket screws and biscuits. The top was fitted immediately, and with great care as the pedestal unit was not stable enough to move until the top was fitted. The finished doors were then fitted to complete the base unit of the desk.

TOP UNIT

The top unit carcass was made from $\frac{1}{2}$in (12mm) finished oak, deep sawn out of $1\frac{1}{2}$in (36mm) stock and thicknessed to size. The sides of the two drawer units were cut to size, and the tops shouldered at the front. Stopped housings for the shelves, dowel holes $\frac{3}{16}$in deep x $\frac{3}{8}$in diameter (5 x 10mm) for the rail ends, and slots for the faced ply back were cut on the inside faces. The bottom rails were cut to size, slotted to take the ply back, and a dowel was formed on the ends on the lathe. The two shelves were cut to size and shouldered at the front, and the ply backs cut to size. All the pieces were sanded to 150grit on the belt and random orbital sanders.

Glue was applied to the slots, housings and dowel holes and the units were assembled, clamped up, checked for square and left to set. Once set, the outside faces were hand-sanded down to 240grit, and varnished in the same way as the base unit.

TOP

The top was cut to size, and the edges rounded over using a radius cutter on the T5 router. Stopped housings were cut in the underside face to take the tops of the drawer unit sides, and a slot was cut to take the ply backs.

BACK

A rail was cut to fit between the two drawer units with a dowel turned on each end and a slot for the ply back cut in the top edge. Dowel holes $3/16$in deep x $3/8$in diameter (5 x 10mm) were drilled on the inside faces of the drawer units. The ply back panel was cut to size and all the pieces sanded to 150grit.

ASSEMBLY

Glue was applied to the slots for the back and the dowel holes. The bottom rail and ply back were fitted between the drawer units, clamped, checked square and left to set. Again, this unit was not stable until the top was fitted. The top was placed flat on the bench with the stopped housings and back slot facing up. Glue was applied to the back slot and housings and the drawer units, joined by the back, were dropped onto the top, locating the tops of the sides and the ply back panels in the relevant housings, then clamped up. Once set the top unit was finished in the same way as the base unit.

FITTING TOP UNIT TO DESK BASE

Biscuit slots were cut in the bottom edges of the top unit sides and corresponding slots in the top of the desk. The desktop was hand-sanded to 240grit, a strip of masking tape was stuck over the back edge where the top unit back rails would glue down, and the top varnished. Once the varnish was cured the masking tape was removed, glue applied to the biscuits, slots and the back rails, then the top unit was clamped to the desktop. Reinforcing screws were drilled through from the underside of the desktop, between the biscuits.

Drilling pockets for screws using Trend jig.

Fitting top unit to desk showing biscuits.

DRAWERS

Chopping the drawer dovetails out.

Checking clearance around drawers using a feeler gauge.

The drawers were made of oak in the usual way, with dovetails front and back and the oak-faced ply bases glued in to the sides, front and back. They were adjusted for size until they ran smoothly in the carcass, stops were fitted, pulls were attached and the running surfaces waxed. The insides of the drawers and pedestals were finished with lemon oil. It seals the surface and has a nice citric scent. I applied the lemon oil from a spray bottle, worked it in and took the surplus off with kitchen tissue.

CONCLUSION

This job took longer than I had thought it would, but it was a bit different, and my client's enthusiasm in the process, and delight with the end result, made it very enjoyable.

Up on a pedestal

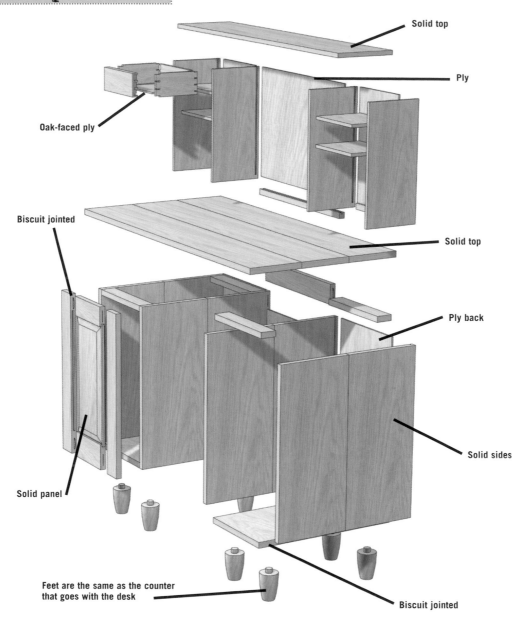

Solid top

Ply

Oak-faced ply

Biscuit jointed

Solid top

Ply back

Solid sides

Solid panel

Feet are the same as the counter
that goes with the desk

Biscuit jointed

The door.

Top drawers – open.

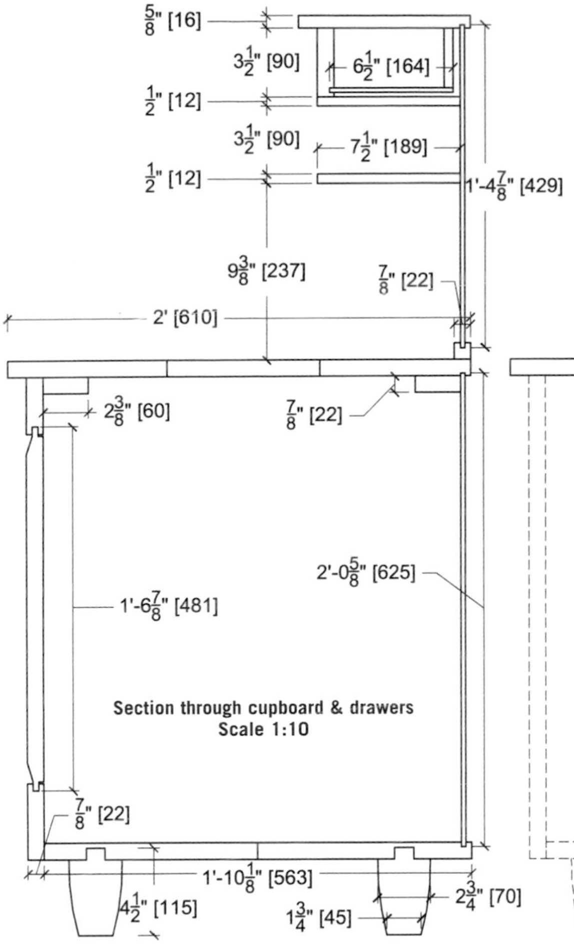
5/8" [16]
3 1/2" [90]
6 1/2" [164]
1/2" [12]
3 1/2" [90]
7 1/2" [189]
1/2" [12]
1'-4 7/8" [429]
9 3/8" [237]
7/8" [22]
2' [610]
2 3/8" [60]
7/8" [22]
2'-0 5/8" [625]
1'-6 7/8" [481]
7/8" [22]
1'-10 1/8" [563]
4 1/2" [115]
1 3/4" [45]
2 3/4" [70]

Section through cupboard & drawers
Scale 1:10

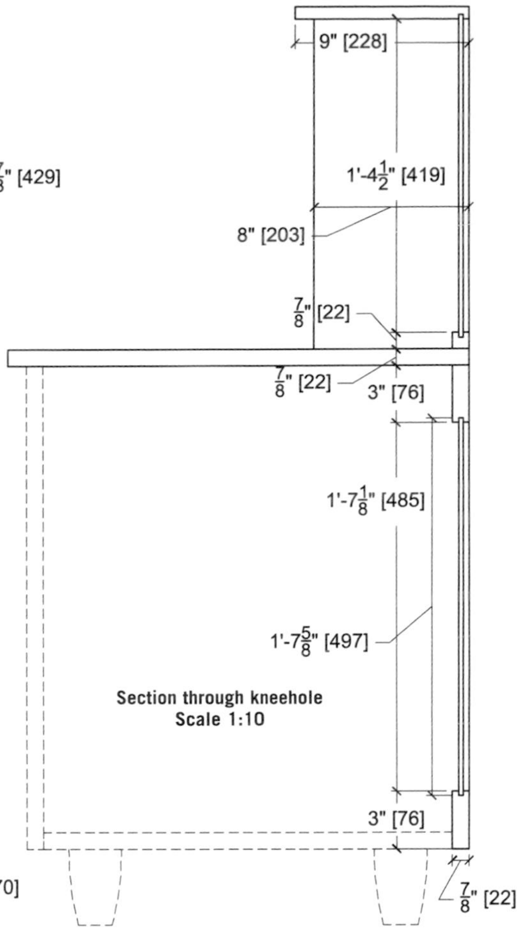
9" [228]
1'-4 1/2" [419]
8" [203]
7/8" [22]
7/8" [22]
3" [76]
1'-7 1/8" [485]
1'-7 5/8" [497]
3" [76]
7/8" [22]

Section through kneehole
Scale 1:10

Plan section through cupboard
Scale 1:10

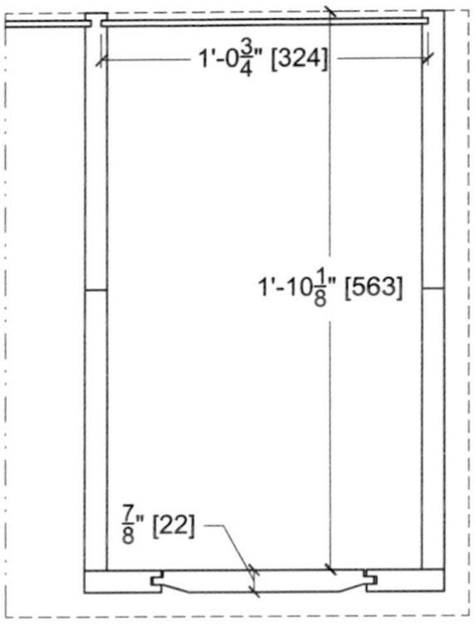
1'-0 3/4" [324]
1'-10 1/8" [563]
7/8" [22]

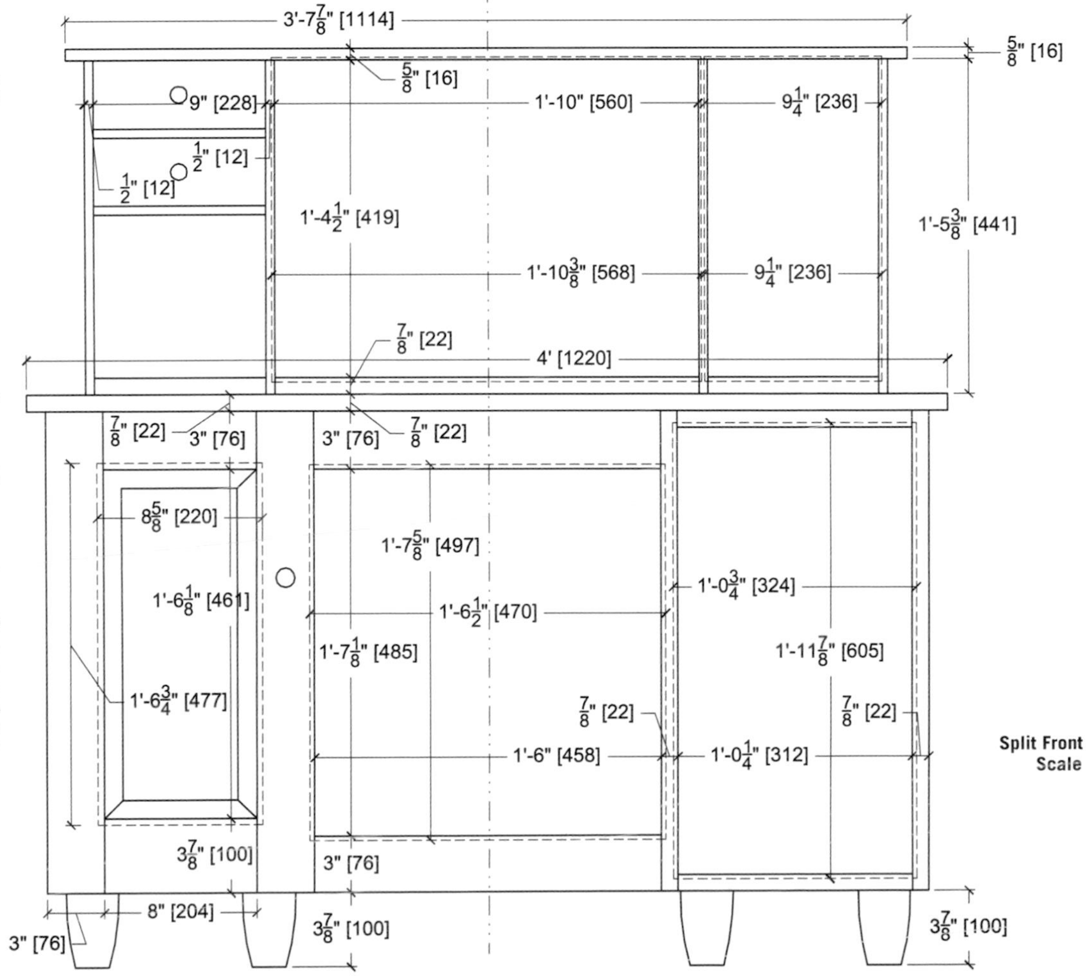
3'-7 7/8" [1114]
5/8" [16]
5/8" [16]
9" [228]
1'-10" [560]
9 1/4" [236]
1/2" [12]
1/2" [12]
1'-4 1/2" [419]
1'-5 3/8" [441]
1'-10 3/8" [568]
9 1/4" [236]
7/8" [22]
4' [1220]
7/8" [22]
3" [76]
3" [76]
7/8" [22]
8 5/8" [220]
1'-7 5/8" [497]
1'-6 1/8" [461]
1'-6 1/2" [470]
1'-0 3/4" [324]
1'-7 1/8" [485]
1'-11 7/8" [605]
1'-6 3/4" [477]
7/8" [22]
7/8" [22]
1'-6" [458]
1'-0 1/4" [312]
3 7/8" [100]
3" [76]
8" [204]
3" [76]
3 7/8" [100]
3 7/8" [100]

Split Front Elevation
Scale 1:10

SEE PAGE 6 FOR NOTES ON USING PLANS

FROM COMMISSION
TO COMPLETION

A Boardroom Suite in Zebrano

Octagonal Boardroom Table

Boardroom Chairs

A BOARDROOM SUITE IN ZEBRANO

Boardroom builds

The following pages describe the various stages involved in the commissioning of a range of prestige boardroom tables and chairs, inspired by high gothic furniture.

The completed boardroom table and chairs.

In the Spring of 2002, a client of long standing called with a very interesting proposition. He had just visited Raby Castle in County Durham, and seen some stunning furniture in the Barons' Hall. The style of the furniture was high gothic, and he had been told the wood was African zebrawood. He was very keen to furnish his company boardroom based on what he had seen – and I was keen to help him.

THE CLIENT

I have worked with this client over several years on a number of major projects and was looking forward to this commission. The client's relaxed and laid-back attitude of 'You can do what I want – I'll wait' was very reassuring.

He likes my general approach, preferring solid timber, simple lines, and attaching great importance to the choice of wood, together we have produced some nice pieces. His discerning individuality and confidence to go for the out-of-the-ordinary is unusual and definitely worth going that extra mile for. Combine this with acceptance of reasonable delivery times and prices, and here is the rare, perfect client: a real pleasure to work with, and never to be taken for granted.

THE CASTLE

The Viking King Cnut – also known as Canute II and 'Emperor of the North', had a manor house here in the eleventh century. But this great fortress, Raby Castle, was built in the fourteenth century for the powerful Neville dynasty, and has been the home of Lord Barnard's family since 1626. It is in the beautiful county of Durham in northern England, set in ornamental gardens and surrounded by rolling parkland, populated by herds of wild deer.

Inside is a wonderful collection of furniture, furnishings and artwork spanning the centuries. It has all the usual facilities and makes a truly worthwhile family visit with interests for all. I have gained much inspiration from the furniture there.

Fourteenth-century Raby Castle in the beautiful county of Durham in northern England.

THE RABY FURNITURE

Tables

The George IV calamander and parcel-gilt octagonal centre table 58in wide x 31in high (1473 x 787mm) and rectangular side table 54in long x 31in high x 32in wide (1371 x 787 x 812mm) reflect the heavy Grecian look found in book-lined rooms in the late eighteenth and early nineteenth centuries.

The inlays, tracery, relief and fretwork in the Old English or gothic style conform to designs found in George Smith's *Collection of Designs for Household Furniture and Interior Decoration* (1808). The contrast in the calamander's marbled figuring reflects the Etruscan and Elizabethan styles popular at that time, while the gilt-work is influenced by the richness of early eighteenth-century French furniture decoration.

Chair

This George IV oak and parcel-gilt chair, around 37in high x 19½in wide x 19¾in deep (940 x 495 x 501mm), was part of a banqueting set of two side chairs and a sofa. With the tables it was included in a large quantity of Grecian gothic furniture commissioned for Raby Castle in the early nineteenth century by William Henry Vane, 3rd Earl of Darlington, 1st Duke of Cleveland and Lord Lieutenant of Durham.

The chairs were also based on designs in the same George Smith reference as the tables, where he extols the use of oak in preference to the then more fashionable mahogany. Similar styles are to be found in his *Cabinet-Maker and Upholsterers Guide* (1826).

Raby George IV calamander and parcel-gilt octagonal centre table.

Raby George IV calamander and parcel-gilt side chair.

THE WOOD

The verbal description of the wood was African zebrawood, which I took to be zebrano. As soon as I got the photos I could see that the furniture he had seen was not made from West African zebrano, but from calamander, an ebony from Asia, unobtainable in the dimensions and quantities required, and out of the question for this project. Fortunately my client was not after copies but an interpretation capturing the essence of what he had seen, and was delighted with the zebrano.

I had never worked with zebrano, having considered it a turner's wood. So I researched it and found it was suitable for the project, being hard, flexible and, though difficult to plane because of interlocked grain and a marked tendency to tear-out, was capable of a fine finish. It is available in big boards, but great care is required in the kilning, as it is prone to surface-cracking and layering; careful inspection before purchase is required.

While researching on the internet I got some translations of German descriptions and was pleased to learn it was suitable for quality furniture and joinery, and interested to find that it was 'largely resistant to mushrooms' – by which I assume fungal attack. According to American sites, zebrano is popular for dashboards on classic Cadillacs.

When I first saw the photos of the furniture I wondered what I was letting myself in for. This style and construction was nothing like my usual work, and I could not see it as my client's taste either. We spoke, I explained my reservations, and he said he wanted my interpretation of the general effect.

Now I had to find out what particular features of the Raby furniture he liked. The essence of the design for him was the general chunky, stable, appearance and the dramatic contrast in the timber. He was not keen on the gilt and marquetry, or any 'fussiness' in the design, and wanted solid wood, not veneer.

OCTAGONAL CENTRE TABLE

Close-up of the octagonal centre table.

This was, to me, the definitive piece. Studying the photos of the original, we both immediately focused on the bottom shelf. It was not necessary to the construction and would get in the way of sitters. The figuring was not in line with that on the top, and we both found it unsightly. So it went. I felt I could construct a table that would be sturdy enough without bottom rail bracing; at its size and weight, this table was not going to be pushed around or messed with in any way.

The next thing we needed to establish was the diameter of the top. Using an 8ft (2.4m) octagonal rug in our sitting room as reference, we tried different diameters in conjunction with our dining chairs, until we came up with a diameter of around 6ft 6in (2m) to seat eight, with plenty of room. The thickness of $1\frac{1}{4}$in (32mm) was taken from the thickness of the top of my oak dining table.

From these two decisions, it was apparent that the table would have to be constructed in such a way that it could be dismantled for transport and installation. Working on one's own, with no immediate neighbours or help conveniently available, and having a first-floor workshop reached by stairs through a standard door, concentrates the mind on such matters wonderfully.

We wanted the table top to be in one piece, and although it would be fairly heavy – at 150–200lb (68–91kg) – I thought I could handle it. We decided on legs of octagonal cross-section to reflect the top shape and assist in the construction.

Now the initial drawings could be created and refinements made as the design progressed. Some increase in my personal strength, together with research on construction techniques and 'knock-down' fixings was required.

SIDE CHAIRS

We had used my dining chairs as a rough guide for the table diameter but they were not of correct proportion for this table. The maximum seat size for the new chairs was found by drawing the table top to scale in my CAD program and measuring it.

The general style of the chairs was taken from the Raby example – chunky, with substantial legs, no leg rails and a straight back. The client wanted them to sit under the top with the backs standing off the perimeter by about 4in (100mm). The seat height was to be standard at about 17½in (440mm) and he chose the back height by referring to chairs in both his house and mine. Octagonal cross-section legs were chosen to link to the table top.

FINDING THE TIMBER

Now that I knew the number of items to be made, and the general dimensions, I could estimate the quantity of timber required. I wanted it all out of the same log, to ensure figure and colour matching, and that would probably mean it would all be the same thickness. After some research with suppliers and detailed examination of the designs, I decided that 1½in (38mm) boards would be most suitable.

The table top was to be as decorative as possible with the distinctive marbled figuring. To get this effect, crown-cut timber was required, but zebrano is usually slash or quarter sawn for stability and to achieve the tramline effect in the figure. Few suppliers could provide what I wanted and the big importers were unwilling to let me select.

It was quite a task to get the quantity, and quality, of timber required in the correct dimensions. In the end, I gave my requirements and specifications to Craft Supplies and with their help purchased a whole log, having gone through it to check quality and ensure there was enough crown-cut, decorative stuff.

DELIVERY AND STORAGE

After I had inspected the timber, it was delivered to my workshop. The boards were 1½in (38mm) thick, 12ft (4m) long and up to 3ft (915mm) wide – not light – and remember, mine is a first-floor workshop. I removed the window casements and, with the help of the deliveryman, pulled it straight in off the lorry. It was sticked and stacked in the workshop and left with the dehumidifiers on, while I took August off and we went to Scotland on holiday.

FINALIZING THE DESIGNS

After the drawings and designs had been fine tuned, a number of 'flying' visits took place, when my client would look over the specific pieces of timber chosen for important features, such as the table tops. We were both very excited about the project – and he loves flying his helicopter.

There were some major practical considerations to this job, not least workshop and machine capacity, access and delivery problems – and even the muscle power required. Just finding the right timber was a major task in itself.

I was warned that the dust was particularly irritant and unpleasant; the table top would present serious finishing problems because of tear-out, and even that the wood had a very unpleasant whiff of the farmyard. This was definitely going to be a challenge.

Raby George IV calamander and parcel-gilt rectangular library table with side chair.

Boardroom builds

TABLE AND CHAIRS SHOWING FIT OF CHAIRS

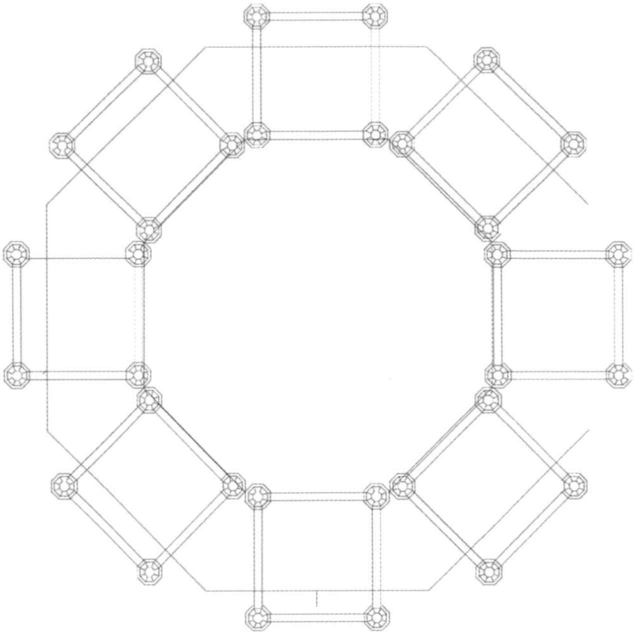

TABLE SIDE VIEW

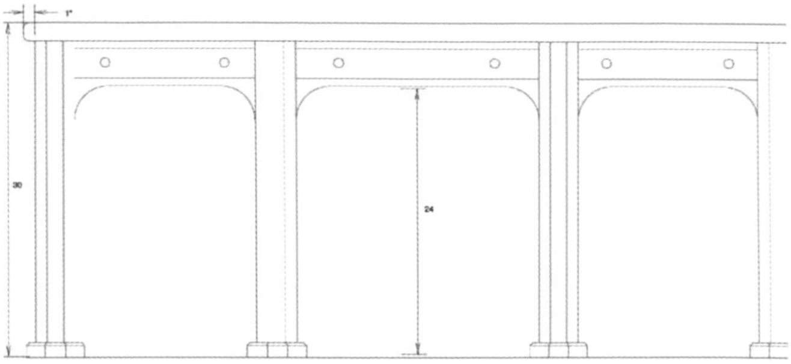

1"

30

24

**SCALE DRAWINGS
OF THE BOARDROOM
CHAIRS**

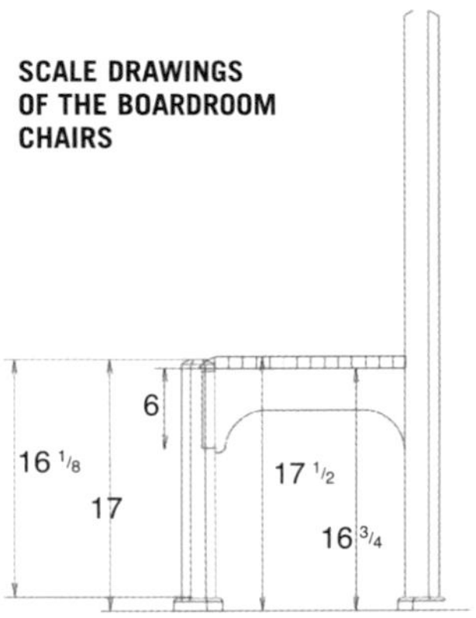

6

16 $\frac{1}{8}$

17

17 $\frac{1}{2}$

16 $\frac{3}{4}$

SIDE

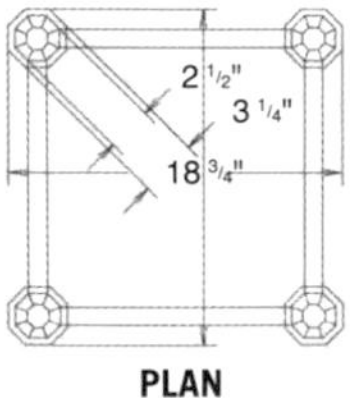

2 $\frac{1}{2}$"

3 $\frac{1}{4}$"

18 $\frac{3}{4}$"

PLAN

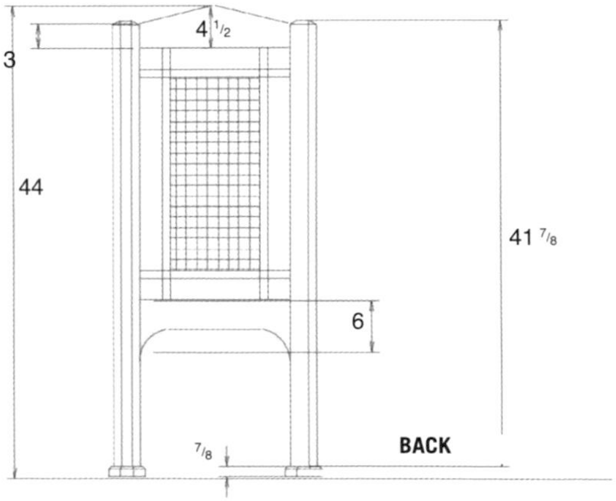

4 $\frac{1}{2}$

3

44

41 $\frac{7}{8}$

6

$\frac{7}{8}$

BACK

OCTAGONAL BOARDROOM TABLE
Table for eight

Now to turn to the practicalities of making the dramatic ocatagonal table in zebrano.

Kevin's version of the Raby table.

DESIGN DETAILS

My client wanted plenty of room at each place on the table so we started by looking at my 6 x 4ft (1830 x 1220mm) dining table and established that about 30in (762mm) per place at the circumference was right. From this, I drew up the top on my CAD program and found a diameter of 6ft (1830mm) gave a side length of approximately 30in (765mm).

We both felt the bottom shelf on the Raby table was unattractive and had limited leg space. We toyed with the idea of a central column supporting the top, although that would need long feet for stability. In the end, we decided to go for the most stable support – a leg at each corner giving plenty of room between sitters. Unlike the Raby table, the legs would be octagonal in cross-section to reflect the shape of the top.

Drawers were required under the top. I pointed out we could have eight drawer fronts, either triangular drawers or four false and four real. We decided on the latter. The shaped bottom drawer rails gave maximum joint strength to the legs with minimum restriction to the knee height. I felt that as each leg was braced three ways, top and bottom drawer rails and frame member, we could dispense with bottom rails on the legs to leave us as much room as possible underneath. I did final working drawings which, after minor alterations, were approved.

PRACTICALITIES

With dimensions and main features of the design now sorted, I had to now consider practicalities. My workshop is on the first floor, accessed by stairs. I work on my own with no near neighbours, and this piece was going to be big and heavy.

TRUE BRIT

I did a rough calculation of the weight of the whole thing at about 350lb (159kg). I believe under current EU regulations that would require seven men to carry it, but as a true Brit I felt I could cope. The top, which my client and I really wanted in one piece, would be more than 150lb (68kg), but I felt that too was manageable. It would go down the stairs, and through the standard 6ft 6in-high (2m) door of the workshop. To be absolutely sure, I did make a mock up in hardboard just to check.

The under frame would be built as two D-shaped, four-legged pieces joined across the middle, the joining pieces running the same way as the grain of the top, for strength. These sub-frames would be manageable in size and weight and would also go down the stairs and through a standard door. I checked the Häfele catalogue and found some suitable fixings: the Maxifix universal connector, a fixed metal dowel which can be screwed into the mortice, and an eccentric cam which is let into the tenon. The dowel fits into a slot in the cam which, when turned, draws up the joint. They are also used on beds to join the head and foot to the sides.

CHAIR POSITIONS

Further drawings on the CAD package established chairs with the required seat size would fit comfortably under the top and between the legs with the chair backs about 4in (100mm) out from the edge of the table.

POSITIONING

To establish relative proportions and positioning, I drew a plan of the room showing a scale plan view of the table and chairs in it, I then checked the door sizes for access. On paper, everything seemed fine – all I had to do now was to get the wood.

SLASH CUT

Zebrano is a large West African tree providing wide, straight, clean boards. The heartwood is a light golden colour with dark brown/black streaks and veining quite similar to ash, but with much more contrast and richer colours. The sapwood is up to 4in (100mm) wide and is a dirty grey colour, meaning it is of little use and leads to high wastage.

Quarter-sawn boards have parallel tramline figuring, crown-cut has much broader, random streaks reminiscent of olive ash. Most of the timber available is 'slash cut', which produces a high proportion of quarter-sawn boards with some crown-cut.

Great care must be taken in the drying process as it has a tendency to surface and end checking, so careful inspection of boards before purchase is recommended. The wood is a little heavier than ash, and is stable with great elastic strength. Thin pieces bend a long way before breaking, all of which is again similar to ash. When wet, the wood smells of the farmyard, and the dust can be an irritant. Interlocked grain makes it a bit of a nightmare to plane, but with sharp tools tear-out is minimized and it can be brought to a fine finish.

I found it moderate to work provided all tools were kept really sharp and dust extractors were in constant use. Its main uses are in turnery, high-class joinery and cabinet making.

SO, WHAT ABOUT THE WOOD?

Until I had seen the photos, I had assumed the timber was zebrano and produced a sample finished on one side with oil and on the other with acrylic varnish. When the original pieces turned out to be in calamander, I quickly established it would not be available at any price in the solid, in the dimensions and quantities required.

Fortunately, my client had fallen for the zebrano and agreed that though the oiled finish looked dirty and yellow, the acrylic-varnished side was crisp and clean with plenty of contrast. Crown-cut boards would provide the dramatic figure required on the table top.

CONDITIONING

Getting hold of the timber was a story in itself, suffice to say I eventually found just what I wanted with the help of Craft Supplies – a whole 12ft (3.7m) log of 1½in (38mm) boards up to 36in (915mm) wide, which had enough crown-cut timber for the top. I checked over each board and selected what I wanted. It was delivered, pulled in through the window, and sticked and stacked in my humidity-controlled workshop to condition. I wanted the timber to be constantly conditioning in the workshop during the whole process.

EXTENDED

The workshop was thoroughly cleaned and tidied to make maximum working space. I have a 6 x 4ft (2 x 1.2m) tongue and groove chipboard, flat, level reference surface laid on the top of the slightly uneven workshop floor for normal work. I extended this to 6 x 6ft (2 x 2m) for the table frame. Machine settings and blade sharpness were checked, and David Charlesworth's advice on machine-planing difficult timbers followed. I polished the backs of my planer blades and put a slight bevel on the back to up the angle, thus increasing the scraping effect of the blades. Hand tools were checked and favourite chisels and planes sharpened. There was method in my madness, as there would not be much spare space for routine tasks once this big piece was under construction in my small workshop.

CUTTING OUT

This is always the most nerve-racking part of the process for me – it's when the final look of the piece is decided. Top priority was the table top so I selected out all the crown-cut boards and chose the best combination and layout, disguising the joint lines by matching the colour and figure and running it through. The drawer fronts are visually part of the top so were chosen carefully to match, as were the pieces for the top and bottom drawer rails.

Next came the pieces to laminate for the legs, remembering that the faceting to make the octagonal shape would expose more figure from the quarter-sawn boards. The under-frame, which would not normally be seen by the sober, was chosen from leftover pieces difficult to match in figure or colour. Once everything was cut out for the table to just over width and length, it was planed and thicknessed, and sticked and stacked in working sequence.

The striking figure of the top.

Planing the top pieces – big bits in a small workshop.

FINISHING

Finishing is not normally done at the beginning of the construction, but when I was thinking through the making process I realized things could be simplified by finishing individual pieces as I went along, rather than waiting until I had large, unwieldy components to deal with. The only danger was in contaminating joints and preventing glue-to-wood contact, but this could be avoided with care.

All the components were hand-planed, scraped and belt-sanded down to 150grit, then random orbital-sanded down to 240grit. Finally they were visually checked and hand-sanded with 240grit on a block. After the first coat of the varnish, the water base tends to raise the grain and I hand-sanded again to 240 or 320grit depending on the grain raising. Three coats of Aquacote water-based matt acrylic varnish were applied to each piece using a varnish roller, rubbing down and de-nibbing between coats with 320grit.

Routing out the leg top dovetail sockets.

LEGS

It had not been possible to source 4in (100mm) dry timber for the legs. So in order to get the best colour and figure match I had decided to go for laminations from my 1½in (38mm) boards of zebrano *(Microberlina brazzavillensis)* – all of which came from the same log.

Three pieces for each leg were cut slightly over length and width and thicknessed to slightly under 1¼in (32mm). They were then offered up and carefully matched for figure and colour. The glue faces were lightly hand-planed to remove the planer ripples and any high spots. The clamps were prepared and the whole area vacuumed to remove any dust and chips. The glue areas were quite large, and the last thing I needed was foreign bodies holding the laminates apart and causing a glue line. Using a 2in (50mm) brush, I applied the Titebond glue to the relevant faces quickly and evenly, and clamped up. I found I could handle the job in two batches of four legs – 12 pieces, eight glues faces – and clamp up using five sash cramps, three under and two over, to achieve even pressure. Once set, the legs were machine planed and thicknessed to an accurate 3½in (90mm) square.

The radial-arm saw was set up in rip mode with a high fence, to cut the corners off down the length and form the octagonal cross-section. The legs were cut to length and the mortices for the bottom drawer rail and the under-frame member routed out and squared off by hand. The leg faces were hand-planed, scraped and sanded down to 240grit, then finished with three coats of matt acrylic.

Squaring off leg mortices.

FEET

The octagonal feet were cut to 4½in (115mm) square and the corners cut off at 45° on the radial-arm saw. The faces and tops were finished on the inverted belt sander and then by hand to 150grit. Chamfers were routed on the tops and finished with a sanding file. They too were hand-finished and varnished with three coats of acrylic varnish. The centre of the top face was covered with masking tape to leave bare wood for gluing.

Fixing the feet accurately was surprisingly difficult. They needed to be seen from above to be positioned accurately in relation to the legs, and then fixed from beneath. In the end, I put a blob of 'I-can't-believe-it's-not nails' glue on the centre of the top face of the foot where the masking tape had been, and placed the leg centrally on it before clamping it in place with a jet clamp. After a 24-hour wait for the glue to set, I removed the clamp, turned the leg over and dovetail screwed the foot to the leg from underneath, filling the screw holes with zebrano plugs. I used three 3in (75mm) screws in an equilateral triangle pattern, drilled at an angle of about 60°, pointing towards the centre of the leg, to prevent pull-out. Incidentally, I have experimented with the 'no nails' glues and found an end grain-to-end grain join very strong, provided it is clamped and left for the full 24 hours' curing time.

Finishing chamfers on feet with sanding file.

Cleaning up the socket.

Sanding faces of feet on inverted belt sander.

FRAMES

The D-shaped frame component was drawn up to
full size on a piece of hardboard to confirm the
measurements of the individual pieces, which had
been taken from the scale drawing in CAD – I only
have so much faith in computers! The under-frame
4 x 1¼in (100 x 32mm) pieces were cut first, and
tenons formed with a dado head on the radial-arm
saw. They were then adjusted by hand to fit the
pre-cut mortices in the legs. Mortices were routed
in the long cross piece, and tenons made on the free
ends of the short cross pieces. The four legs, long
cross pieces and short cross pieces were dry
assembled and the drawer rail lengths checked.
The drawer rails were cut to length and width and
the tenons formed on the bottom rails using the
dado head on the radial-arm saw. Once the tenons
had been cut, the undersides were cut out to shape
and the edges rounded over on the router table.
The shaped underside of the bottom rails were
sanded using a drum sander on the radial-arm saw.
Then the rails and frame members were finished
with three coats of acrylic varnish.

How the two frame halves fit together.

Routing the mortices.

Knock–down fitting and dry dovetail.

ASSEMBLY

First the two centre legs were glued and clamped up
to their bottom drawer rail. The two short frame and
one long frame members were then clamped to those
two legs. Finally, each end leg was added by
attaching it with its bottom drawer rail. Great care
was taken to ensure all the legs were vertical in each
direction, and the clamps were padded with pieces
of carpet to prevent damage to the finished surfaces.

At this point, the dovetails were cut on the top rails
using the band saw and offered up to the leg tops,
which were marked with a scalpel to position the
sockets. These were routed out freehand to the
correct depth and close to the knifed edge using
my T5 router and a long two-flute straight cutter,
then finally trimmed to fit with a paring chisel. The
top rails were finished, glued and tapped home over
the middle legs.

D-FRAMES

The two D-frames were joined at each end by the drawer rails and in the centre by the cross pieces. The top drawer rails were a simple, dry dovetail joint with a screw through the tail into the leg to act as a removable fixing pin. The bottom rails were fitted with a Häfele fastener at each end to pull the dry mortice and tenon join up tight. The centre cross pieces were each fitted with two Häfele fasteners at each end and butt jointed to the long rail. The top of the frame was checked with a long straight edge and brought flat and level with a jackplane. Expansion plates were then fitted for the top.

FALSE DRAWERS

Before the top rails were tapped home on the ends where the false drawer fronts would be, biscuit slots were cut to locate the false drawer fronts. These were cut in the top face of the bottom rails and the under face of the top rails. Corresponding slots were cut in the top and bottom edges of the false fronts, which were then fitted and trimmed to exact size. The biscuits were not glued, and small packing pieces were fitted at the back to locate the false drawer fronts with similar clearances to the true drawer fronts. Once I was happy with the false drawer fronts, the top rails' dovetails were glued into the legs. Before fitting, the false drawer fronts had been drilled for pulls and finished.

DRAWERS

The drawer runners and kickers were rebated to include guides, and glued and screwed into position on the under-frame between the relevant legs. The individual pieces of the drawer carcasses were cut to size and fitted in the usual way, before being carefully marked for identification. The holes for the pulls were drilled in the fronts but were not fitted.

A cutting gauge was used to mark the width and length of the dovetails on the relevant pieces, and the fronts and sides had housings cut to take the bases. Double pairs of sides were taped together, the tails marked with a sharp pencil, cut out on the bandsaw and cleaned up with a sharp chisel.

Each side was offered up to its front and the pins marked with a scalpel. A router with a straight cutter was set to the correct depth, and the side fence was adjusted to cut out the majority of the waste to form the pins. Final adjustments were made with a paring chisel. The inside faces of the drawer carcass pieces were then sanded, and the drawers assembled and glued up. The oak-faced MDF bases were glued into the slots in the fronts and sides, and glued and screwed to the backs.

The completed drawers were checked for square and wind and left to set, before being fitted into their relevant places in the under-frame, with stops. The fronts were sanded and finished.

One of the four drawers.

Fitting runners for the drawers.

PULLS

Drawer pulls were turned on the lathe out of zebrano, which I found very nice to turn. As usual, I took full advantage of my sizing tools and profiler gauge. The pulls were finished and fitted to all the drawer fronts.

TOP

The final part of the construction was the top, which will take a lot less time to explain how to do it than it actually took to do! It comprised seven pieces of edge-jointed timber. I laid out the boards on the floor before hand-planing all the edges to fit. The final shape was chalked on and the positions of the biscuits marked, ensuring they would not be exposed when the final trimming was done, especially at the corners. Initially, I assembled three separate sections, one of three pieces and two of two pieces. This reduced the panic of adjusting the joints during the open time of the glue. I then glued and clamped all three sections together to make the complete top.

With a bit of a struggle it was placed upside down on the frame, which was padded with carpet offcuts to prevent damage to what would become the glorious top surface.

Rounding over the top edge.

MARKING

After marking the exact and final shape, it was sawn out by hand ⅛in (3mm) outside the line. I clamped a straight edge on each side in turn and, with a 2in (50mm) deep cutter on my T9 router, trimmed accurately to the line, using an up/down shear cutter to avoid edge feathering and to achieve a good finish. The underside was planed flat and belt sanded to a finish. The edges were then belt-sanded, using a parallel fence to keep at right-angles to the top, before they were rounded over with a radius cutter. The surface and edges were sanded to a finish, given three coats, and left to set. The top was then turned over to bring the correct face up, positioned correctly, and fixed to the expansion plates on the under-frame. I double-checked the length of the screws to make sure they did not go right through, and that they went into the correct slot to allow for movement.

The top surface was now flattened and finished with plane, scraper plane, scraper, belt sander, random orbital sander, hand-sanding block, blood, sweat and tears. It was given a coat of varnish, and minutely checked for blemishes, which were removed. The process was repeated until I was happy, then it was given five thin coats, a rubbing down and de-nibbing between coats. The result was quite stunning and worth the considerable effort.

Top laid out.

Flattening and finishing the top.

FINAL FINISHING

The whole piece was examined carefully for blemishes and marks. All the visible surfaces were cut back with a Scotchbrite grey pad and given two more thin coats of Aquacote. It was left for seven days to fully cure.

MOVING OUT

My first major problem was to get the table into the cottage to photograph it for *Furniture & Cabinet Making* magazine. We made a skid lined with blankets, and used it to slide the well-wrapped-up top on its edge down a scaffold board placed over the stairs. Having cleared the dining room, we set the table up there and took the pictures. It was then dismantled and stored in my wife Yvonne's studio to await my client's curtain-sider lorry.

DISH SHAPE

The table was going from me into storage until the boardroom had been refurbished, and I wanted the top fixed to the frame to make sure it wasn't left leaning against a wall for a couple of months, where it would develop a nice dish shape! I had established it would fit into the lorry and go into the boardroom in one piece. The only place I could have it assembled and ready to go was in my garage.

LIFT OFF

I had arranged for two chaps to come down with the lorry. The night before I woke up thinking 'I hope the lorry has a drop tail board for us to carry it up.' I checked first thing the next morning and it didn't, but it was already on route. Panic stations! I used the two old doors as a platform and the two pieces of an aluminium ladder as skids underneath. We lifted one end of the ladders up on the tail board, then lifted the others level and the doors with the table on top were slid home along the ladders on to the lorry.

IN CONCLUSION

This was an exciting piece to make. My client was very involved in the design, and we were both delighted with the end result. It was probably about the limit in size and weight for a single piece in my one-man workshop, but it is surprising how problems can be solved when we really put our minds to them. A perfect piece for the maxim: 'Don't start until you know what you are doing!'

The finished table.

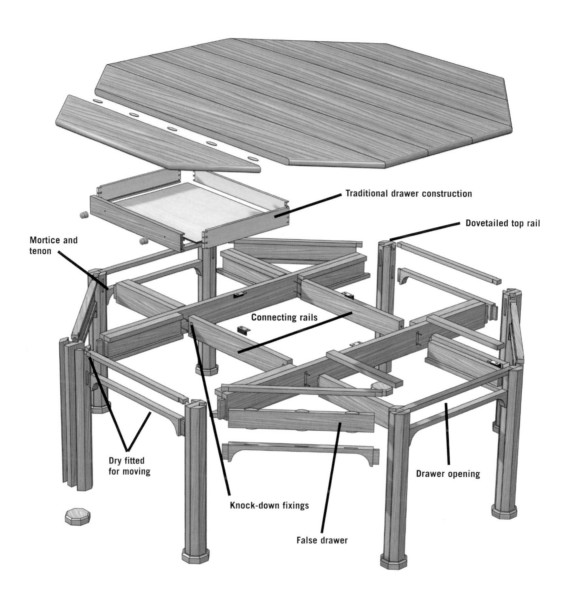

Traditional drawer construction

Dovetailed top rail

Mortice and tenon

Connecting rails

Dry fitted for moving

Knock-down fixings

Drawer opening

False drawer

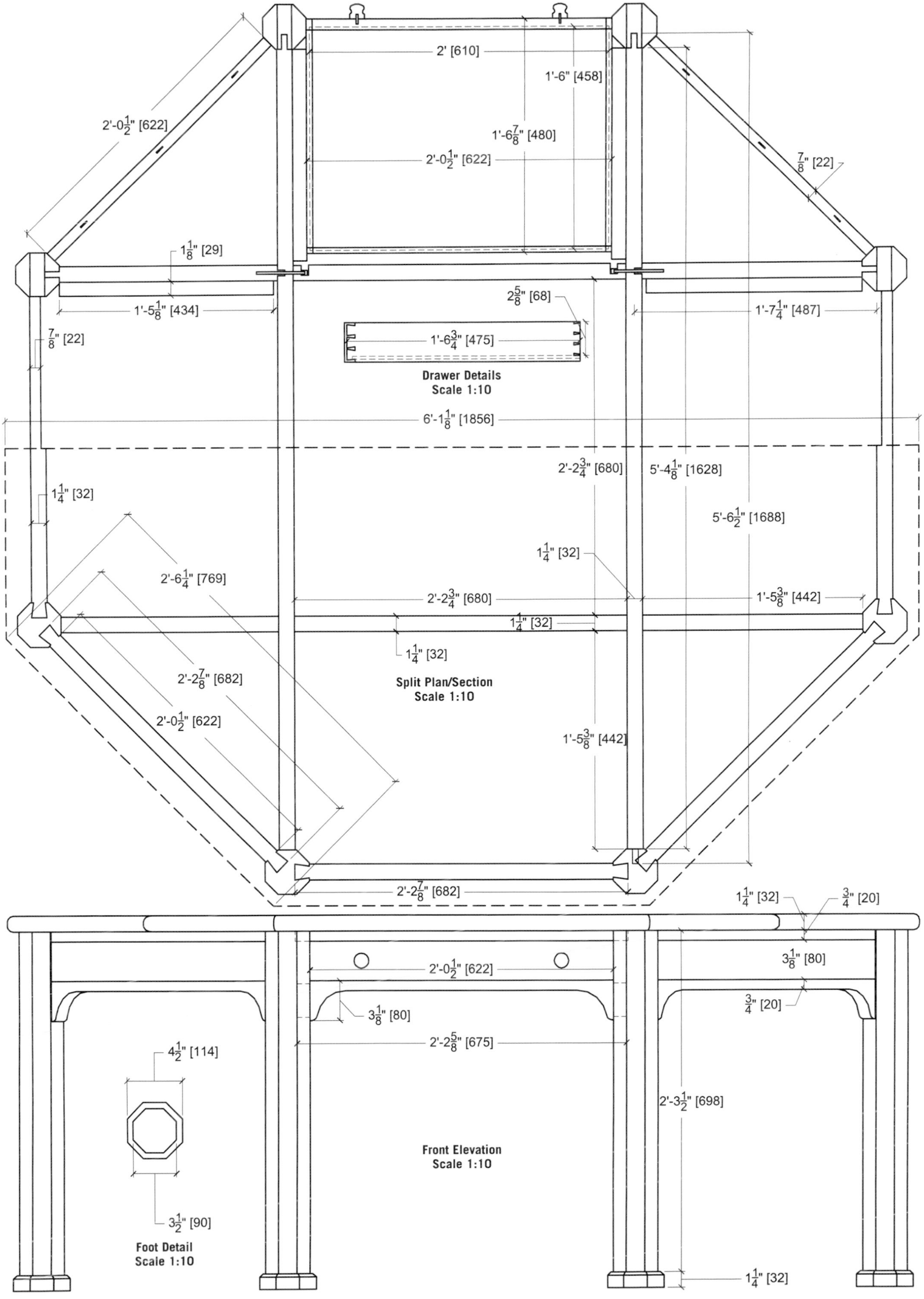

2' [610]

1'-6" [458]

2'-0½" [622]

1'-6⅞" [480]

2'-0½" [622]

7/8" [22]

1⅛" [29]

1'-5⅛" [434]

2⅝" [68]

1'-7¼" [487]

7/8" [22]

1'-6¾" [475]

Drawer Details
Scale 1:10

6'-1⅛" [1856]

2'-2¾" [680]

5'-4⅛" [1628]

5'-6½" [1688]

1¼" [32]

1¼" [32]

2'-6¼" [769]

2'-2¾" [680]

1'-5⅜" [442]

1¼" [32]

1¼" [32]

2'-2⅞" [682]

Split Plan/Section
Scale 1:10

2'-0½" [622]

1'-5⅜" [442]

2'-2⅞" [682]

1¼" [32]

¾" [20]

3⅛" [80]

2'-0½" [622]

¾" [20]

3⅛" [80]

2'-2⅝" [675]

4½" [114]

2'-3½" [698]

3½" [90]

Foot Detail
Scale 1:10

Front Elevation
Scale 1:10

1¼" [32]

SEE PAGE 6 FOR NOTES ON USING PLANS

BOARDROOM CHAIRS
Seating the board

This set of eight chairs complement the zebrano boardroom table perfectly.

Pair of chairs – one back, one front.

Two chairs from the front.

I had been fortunate enough to receive a commission from a client of long standing to furnish a whole boardroom in zebrano. It came at a good time for me as I had just about finished all the alterations to and furniture for our new cottage, had only a few months' work on the books and was looking for a challenge. The principle piece was an octagonal boardroom centre table, featured on pages 115–125. These were the chairs which would enable the board to be seated.

DESIGN

The inspiration for the whole design had been a collection of nineteenth-century high gothic furniture my client had seen at Raby Castle in County Durham, see page 110. He did not want copies but a modern interpretation to give an imposing, dramatic, solid, stable look to the room, with modern clean lines and no fussiness.

The George IV side chairs he had seen, in oak and parcel gilt, were not part of a set with the octagonal table but, like the table, were based on designs found in George Smith's *Designs for Household Furniture and Interior Decoration* (1808). They were part of a banqueting set that had been ordered at the same time as the table and other furniture in the early nineteenth century.

Much in the same style as the table, they were very ornate with a lot of raised-gilt work, but they would be a suitable start point for the chairs I was to make. My client wanted my cleaner, simpler, modern interpretation while keeping the stable, solid look. When not in use the chairs were to stand with the legs under the table and the backs about 4in (100mm) back from the edge.

Prepared timber for the chairs sticked and stacked to condition.

I played on the computer CAD program and arrived at the maximum seat width, with the front legs just meeting under the table. To keep the chunky look that my client liked I kept the seats square, with no taper to the back. The seat height, including upholstery, was standard at 17½in (442mm).

An octagonal cross-section and octagonal feet to the legs matched the table, with chamfered tops to add finishing detail. A taller back gave more weight, balancing the bulk of the table, with an inset back frame to take a push-in panel, upholstered on both sides in black velvet; drop-in foam padded seats completed the design.

TIMBER
I had had a lot of trouble sourcing suitable quantities of the right quality and dimensions of zebrano but eventually found just what I wanted with the help of Craft Supplies. I had initially tried to obtain thicknesses of 1, 2, 3 and 4in (25, 50, 75 and 100mm) but had been unable to find kiln-dried zebrano any thicker than 50mm.

In the end I bought a whole 12ft (3.7m) log of 1½in (38mm) boards up to 3ft (915mm) wide, with enough crown-cut timber for a dramatic table top, and plenty of quarter-sawn timber for the chairs.

I felt that the advantage of achieving the entire boardroom set from one log, thus ensuring consistency in the properties of the timber, especially the colour and figure, outweighed the extra work in laminating the legs and deep sawing for the chair rails.

I checked over each board and selected what I wanted. It was delivered, pulled in through the window, and sticked and stacked to condition in my humidity-controlled workshop while I went on holiday. This was going to be a long job and I wanted the timber to be constantly conditioning in the workshop during the whole making process.

ECONOMICAL CUTTING OUT
I decided to cut out all the timber for the table and chairs in one go, calculating that if I started with the biggest pieces for the table and worked progressively down to the smaller pieces for the chairs, I could minimize waste on an already expensive timber.

I always put a lot of thought into this process as it has such an effect on the final look. The most important part was matching the crown-cut pieces for the table top. Once that was done I completed the table pieces and began to cut the chairs from the straighter-figured, quarter-sawn boards and the smaller pieces left over.

Once the cutting out was completed, I decided to deep saw the wood for the chair side rails, using the offcuts for the table drawer carcasses, and face and thickness all the wood to make sure there were no surprises in the figuring or colour on pieces that were to be joined. Having so much timber in so many pieces in my small workshop was quite an organizational challenge, but all went well and careful marking and checking saw me through. Once it was all done, the wood was stacked in working sequence, chairs on top of the table.

I had prepared the planer blades, following David Charlesworth's advice, by polishing the backs and putting a slight back bevel on to increase the scraping effect and reduce tear-out.

BATCH WORK
Chairs are ideal projects for batch production, with a high ratio of joints on small pieces and repeat cuts at the same machine settings. The argument is even stronger for a set of eight chairs. It can be a bit boring doing 60+ repeat cuts but the setting-up time is minimized and, providing the cut is accurate, time is saved and costs are cut.

The essence of batch production is care and organization. Accurate cutting lists, careful preparation, sequencing of actions and use of rods and jigs for repeat measurements and actions are essential. Machines should be checked for accuracy of settings, fences, adjustment locks, blade sharpness and the like.

Showing extra braces from leg to seat brace.

STARTING CONSTRUCTION

I carefully checked that I had the correct number – and sometimes an insurance spare – of each item, see 'Batch Work' panel on previous page. The various pieces were stacked to a known number high and the stacks counted; indeed I became quite paranoid, wandering round the workshop counting little piles of wood and making chalk marks on them.

All the cuts at a particular machine setting were made at the same time, the measurements of the first one off double-checked, and subsequent random checks made, so that I didn't make 60+ mistakes – in other words, I made haste slowly.

Careful planning ensured that all the cuts at any particular setting were made before that setting was changed. There was a certain satisfaction in doing this repetitive work accurately but I prefer the constant individual challenges of normal one-off progressive making.

Cutting mortices on planer slot morticer attachment.

Drilling the holes for the turned end dowels of the back frame in the seat back rail using a plunge router with a stop clamped to the fence.

LEGS

The pairs of prepared front and back leg pieces were carefully matched for colour and figure, and where possible the figure was taken through the joint line to mask it. The tops of both the front and back legs would be visible so the end-grain figure was also important. This timber was relatively easy to match up, the soft joint glue line being virtually lost in the strongly lined figuring.

The joining faces were hand-planed to remove the planer ripples, and a tad more taken from the middle of both faces so that, when clamped, the ends pulled up tight and were under tension, to allow for the possible shrinkage caused by future extra drying out – wood loses moisture more readily from the end grain. Titebond was spread evenly on one of the meeting faces, and the legs were clamped up in sash cramps, four at a time, and left to set.

The joining pieces had been cut oversize to allow for facing, squaring and thicknessing, which was now carried out. Then the legs were cut to length and $2\frac{1}{2}$in (63mm) square section.

With the ripsaw blade set to 45° the bulk of the waste could be cut off the corners of the leg lengths to make the octagonal cross-section, leaving enough spare material to plane and thickness the new faces. This was done with care to ensure exactly the same amount came off each side, leaving octagonal legs of the correct length with equal faces.

Unfortunately, the legs were too thick to fit the Trend mortice and tenon attachment to form the leg mortices, so the mortices for the seat rails and the top were marked and cut on the planer morticing attachment. Using the same cutter and central setting, the dowel holes were cut in the back legs for the back frame dowel ends.

Fitting tenon.

Close-up of seat rail tenons to leg mortices.

CONSERVATION
My client was concerned about the conservation aspect of using this timber but was reassured by Craft Supplies' policy of buying from selected sustainable sources and making every effort to be ecologically sympathetic.

TOP BEVELS
The leg ends were fine-sanded lightly on the radial-arm saw disc sander attachment to ensure they were flat and true. Then the saw blade was replaced and raised, set to a suitable angle and a stop set to locate on the centre of the leg. This allowed all eight cuts to be made in rotation, to form the bevels, with the legs held against the fence.

I chose the angle by eye, keeping it quite shallow. Needless to say, several trial runs were made first, using the offcuts from cutting the legs to length, until I was satisfied with the look. I used a fine, sharp, TCT blade to minimize finishing. The leg top now had eight bevels and a centre flat.

DOWEL HOLES FOR FEET
I had decided to dowel the feet to the legs with 3 x ⅜in (10mm) dowels, but had to add a fourth centre dowel to help line up the octagonal faces of the legs and feet. The holes had to be drilled accurately at right-angles and the legs were too long to go under my drill press, so I fitted a brad-point 10mm drill into the slot morticer chuck, marked the centre and perimeter holes on the leg ends, and drilled the dowel holes on the morticer. The back legs were supported on a roller stand to avoid any strain on the relatively small morticer table.

FINISHING LEGS
With the leg work done, the faces were finished with a fine-set jackplane, cabinet scraper and sanding blocks. I had decided not to use the belt sander for fear of losing the definition and/or line on the eight narrow faces.

It took a lot longer but was worth it for the result. There was some tear-out, which took a bit of removing, but the scraper did the trick. Sanding was as light as possible, achieved by using a hard block, again to protect the edges of the narrow faces.

Next, the bevels were finished very carefully with a hand scraper to preserve their definition. Again, this called for a very light and careful sanding with 320grit on a hard block – it was very easy to lose the line and shape of the shallow bevels because the sanding block was bigger than the area of the bevel, and it was difficult to keep the reference.

It all took a long time but was eventually completed to my satisfaction. The finished legs were stacked carefully out of the way.

FEET
The octagonal feet were ⅜in (10mm) wider than the legs, ⅞in (22mm) thick with a chamfer on the edges. They were initially cut square and the corners cut off on the radial-arm saw to form the octagonal. The faces were finished on the sanding disc attachment, then the bevel cut on the router table using a 45° cutter with a guide bearing. The faces were finished with a scraper and sanding block.

The centres of the feet were marked and a hole drilled on the pillar drill fitted with a 10mm brad-point bit, to take a loose dowel. The legs were held, end up, in the vice and dowel points fitted in the pre-drilled holes.

A dry dowel was fitted in the centre hole and the feet offered up to the legs, centred on the dry dowel. They were lined up carefully by eye with the leg faces and pressed on to the dowel points to leave a marked centre for the purpose of drilling the dowel holes in the feet. The dowel holes were drilled, again on the pillar drill.

I decided that it would be easier to varnish the feet and legs separately as the varnish would not contaminate any joints, so they were not joined at this point.

This method of joining the feet to the legs was very time-consuming and the joint was probably over-engineered for possible future stresses. For the table legs and feet I decided to use three countersunk screws in a dovetail pattern, with the feet positioned and located using No Nails glue. That method was very satisfactory and, if doing this again, I would use it on these feet, rather than on the dowels.

SEAT RAILS
The seat rails and tops were cut to length and the dowel holes for the back frame's turned dowel ends were drilled in the under-edge of the tops and the top face of the back seat rails. The pieces were held in the bench vice and the holes cut with a plunge router; a stop was used on the side fence to locate the holes.

The seat rail tenons were formed on the Trend M+T jig. A slightly undersized cutter was used to give a 'fat' tenon which I could tailor with a shoulder plane to fit each mortice – oversize tenons are easy to adjust but undersize are not!

A $^5/_{32}$in (4mm) slot was cut in each rail; the seat braces, joined with Tanseli wafers, would fit into these. The braces would also support the seat panel.

Next, the undersides of the rails were shaped on the bandsaw, and finished on the drum sander attachment on the radial-arm saw. The underside edges and topside outer edge were rounded over on the router table with a radius cutter.

TOPS
The tops were shaped on the bandsaw and the tenons cut on the Trend jig after the seat rails so that only the length of the tenon needed to be adjusted. The top edges were finished with a jackplane and sanding block.

BACK FRAMES
The back frame pieces were cut to length and the ends shouldered on the radial-arm saw. Using a sizing tool, the ends were turned on the lathe to form dowels. The dowels were left slightly oversize and adjusted at the time of fitting with a dowel pop – a piece of $^1/_4$in (6mm) mild steel with accurate holes cut in it for dowels to be tapped, pushed, or 'popped' through for accurate sizing. They can be used to make your own dowels from scrap wood pieces.

Next, the pieces were half lapped to form a centre rectangle to take the upholstered back panel. The half laps were cut on the radial-arm saw using multiple passes, with the blade set to the correct depth, and stops set on the fence to ensure that the female halvings were cut tight. The male halvings could be adjusted slightly with a plane, scraper or sanding block, and tapped in for a perfect fit.

Using the router table and a straight cutter, stopped rebates were cut in the forward edges for the back panel. Glue was applied to the half laps, the frames assembled and clamped and, when set, the rebates were finished square with a paring chisel. The frames were then scraped and block-sanded to a finish.

Chair clamped up showing 'spreading' jet clamp adjusting diagonal.

FINISHING

The workshop was cleaned and tidied and all the pieces were laid out carefully, checked over, dents and marks removed, and finally sanded to 320grit.

I used acrylic varnish, which dries fast, enabling several coats to be applied in one day; it hardens quickly to a tough finish. In this case, a matt look was required.

The first coat can dry quite quickly and get tacky while it is still being worked but adding 10% water or dampening the piece first can cure this.

As usual, the first coat raised the grain and all was sanded back with 320grit to a smooth surface. Zebrano has an open grain and this coat was sanded back quite hard to act as a grain filler. After curing, a second coat was applied and also rubbed back to a smooth surface with 320grit abrasive. A third coat was applied and treated in the same way.

FINISHING CONSIDERATIONS

Assembled chairs are a pain to finish, there being very few opportunities to 'run off' a brush or pad, resulting in build up at joins, uneven finishing and difficult de-nibbing and rubbing down. I prefer to finish the individual pieces and assemble carefully afterwards. Chair joints are relatively easy to protect from varnish contamination that would weaken glue joints – which should be wood to wood. All the joints were check fitted dry and any final adjustments made.

I applied the acrylic finish using a Harris varnish roller, which allows a much longer working period without lifting the layer, and I found it very successful. As the varnish is water-based, the roller is easily washed and reused.

Components of chairs curing after finishing.

Sizing round tenons with a dowel plate.

Dowel points in leg holes with foot about to be offered.

ASSEMBLY

First, the feet were fitted to the legs. Titebond was applied to the dowel holes and the loose dowels tapped into the legs. Then the feet were pushed onto the dowels and a jet clamp, with its greater reach, was used from the centre of the leg top to the centre of the underside of the foot. The leg top was protected with carpet pads.

Next, the backs were assembled. Titebond glue was painted on the insides of the mortices of the tops and back seat rails, and the back frame dowel holes, so that the glue would be pushed into the joint when it was assembled, giving as little glue ooze as possible. The backs were assembled and clamped, and diagonals checked for square and left to set.

Pads of carpet pieces were again put under wooden blocks to prevent marking of the finish by the clamp jaws. The front legs and seat rail were assembled in a similar manner.

Back frame clamped up.

Finishing leg faces with cabinet scraper.

'Tapping' the corner seat braces in with a 2¹⁄₂lb club hammer.

SEAT AND LEG BRACES

At this point, a front was offered up to a back and a chair assembled using dry joints on the side rails. I measured the seat braces and cut them all from the pieces I had cut out from the seat rails when forming the under-curved shape.

A ⁵⁄₃₂in (4mm) slot was cut in each end to take a Tanseli wafer; this will join it to the seat rails. When I dry fitted the seat braces I realized I could add a further brace from the underside of the seat rails to the legs. These braces were cut from scrap and drilled and countersunk for the screws which would fit them to the legs just under the seat and the underside of the seat braces.

Gluing the side rail mortices and clamping up in a similar way to the fronts and backs saw each chair assembled. While the glue was soft, the seat braces were tapped home with a club hammer. There was little swing room and the heavy hammer did the trick far better than a lighter hammer would have done.

The chair was stood on my flat, true, reference surface and, where necessary, my trusty white rubber mallet was applied to ensure all the legs were touching the floor. A small jet clamp, with the jaws reversed to make it into a 'spreader', was applied against the relevant leg braces to correct the diagonal while the chair set, where necessary. The leg braces were now glued and screwed into position.

FINAL FINISHING

The chairs were checked very carefully all over for any marking and rubbed down with a Scotchbrite red pad as necessary.

A final very thin coat of varnish was applied over all with a cloth-covered pad to ensure an even finish. To prevent runs and build-up at the joints, the pad was damp rather than wet with varnish. To matt it down, this coat was cut back with a Scotchbrite grey pad.

SEAT AND BACK PANELS

The seat panels were cut from beech-faced $\frac{1}{2}$in (12mm) five ply. As they were to be a drop-in fit, due allowance was made for the thickness of the velvet with which they would be upholstered. The back panels were to be a push fit from the front and were cut to fit much tighter.

Chair awaiting upholstery.

UPHOLSTERY

The seat and back panels and the velvet my client had chosen were sent to my usual upholsterer with instructions on what was required. They were returned and fitted and the client came down to see the finished chairs.

He was delighted and the chairs were delivered. However, after they had been in use for a short time he was not happy with the foam seats, which he felt were too soft and 'bottomed' onto the seat panel. This was uncomfortable and effectively also reduced the height of the seats.

The seats were returned and I went to the foam supplier to discuss the problem. He told me the foam that had been used was covering foam, to go over hard foam in a layer construction, and that my seats needed a denser foam.

I ordered the foam, cut to the exact size using a seat panel as a pattern, and it was a relatively simple matter to remove the top covers carefully, change the foam, and re-staple the top covers into position. They were a definite improvement and I confidently returned the seats to my client.

CONCLUSION

I hate it when something goes wrong, especially for such an important client, on such a big project, into which I had put so much effort. But the problem over the seats taught me a lesson – I should have been more closely involved in the choice of foam rather than leaving it to the upholsterer. However, the problem was dealt with quickly and to my client's satisfaction, and he is pleased with the final result.

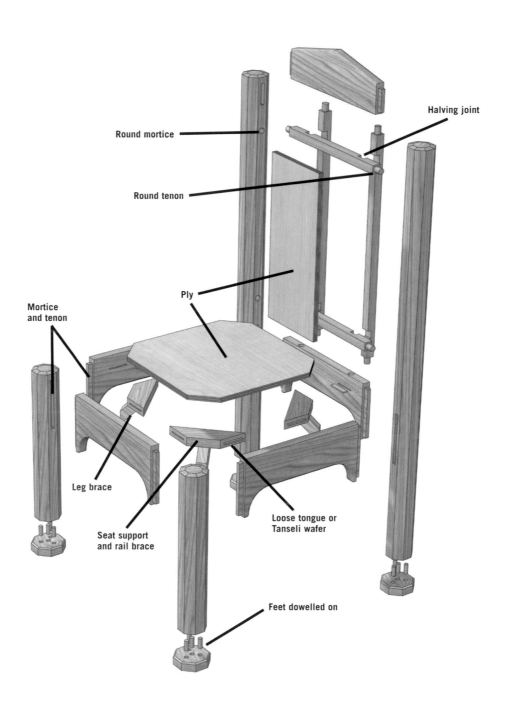

Round mortice

Halving joint

Round tenon

Ply

Mortice
and tenon

Leg brace

Seat support
and rail brace

Loose tongue or
Tanseli wafer

Feet dowelled on

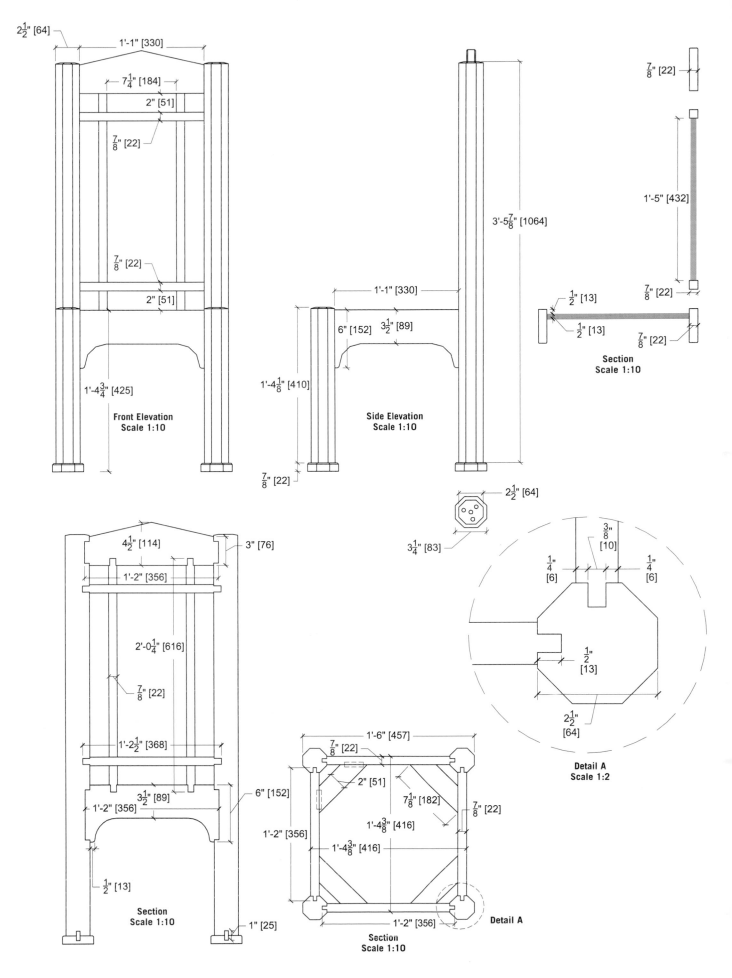

2½" [64]

1'-1" [330]

7¼" [184]

2" [51]

⅞" [22]

⅞" [22]

2" [51]

1'-4¾" [425]

Front Elevation
Scale 1:10

1'-1" [330]

6" [152]

3½" [89]

3'-5⅞" [1064]

1'-4⅛" [410]

⅞" [22]

Side Elevation
Scale 1:10

⅞" [22]

1'-5" [432]

⅞" [22]

½" [13]

½" [13]

⅞" [22]

Section
Scale 1:10

2½" [64]

3¼" [83]

4½" [114]

3" [76]

1'-2" [356]

2'-0¼" [616]

⅞" [22]

1'-2½" [368]

3½" [89]

1'-2" [356]

6" [152]

½" [13]

Section
Scale 1:10

1" [25]

1'-6" [457]

⅞" [22]

2" [51]

7⅛" [182]

⅞" [22]

1'-4⅜" [416]

1'-4⅜" [416]

1'-2" [356]

1'-2" [356]

Detail A

Section
Scale 1:10

⅜" [10]

¼" [6]

¼" [6]

½" [13]

2½" [64]

Detail A
Scale 1:2

SEE PAGE 6 FOR NOTES ON USING PLANS

SUPPLIERS UK

ARNOLD LAVER TIMBERWORLD
Bramall Lane, Sheffield S2 4RJ, UK
Tel: 01142 230300
www.timberworld.co.uk
Timber, sheet materials and ancillary products

AXMINSTER POWER TOOL CENTRE
Axminster, Devon EX13 5PH, UK
Tel: 0800 371822
www.axminster.co.uk
Extensive range of tools, machinery, accessories
and consumables

BARFORDS AQUACOTE
Alan Barford, 17 Ardley Works, London Road
Billericay CM12 9HP, UK
Tel: 01277 622050
www.barfords.com
Aquacote acrylic varnish

CLARKE INTERNATIONAL
Hemnal Street, Epping, Essex CM16 4LG, UK
Tel: 01992 565300
www.clarkeinternational.com
Major supplier and manufacturer of woodworking
hand and power tools

DEWALT POWER TOOLS
210 Bath Road, Slough, Berkshire SL1 3YD, UK
Tel: 01753 567055
www.dewalt.co.uk
Wide range of high-performance industrial
portable electric power tools and accessories

METABO
25 Majestic Road, Nursling Industrial Estate
Southampton, Hampshire SO16 0YT, UK
Tel: 02380 732000
www.metabo.co.uk
Woodworking machinery and power tools

BOSCH
Robert Bosch Power Tools
PO Box 98, Uxbridge UB9 5HN, UK
Tel: 08102 414131
www.boschpowertools.co.uk
Power tools and accessories

SCREWFIX DIRECT
FREEPOST (within UK only), Yeovil
Somerset BA22 8BF, UK
Tel: 0500 414141
www.screwfix.com
Online supplier of trade tools, hardware products
and materials

JET TOOLS
Unit 10, Weycroft Ave
Axminster
Devon, EX13 5XU, UK
Tel: 0845 6040064
www.jet.uk.com
Power tools, machinery and workshop equipment

TREND ROUTING TECHNOLOGY
Odhams Trading Estate, St Albans Road
Watford WD24 7TR, UK
Tel: 01923 224681
www.trendmachinery.co.uk
Routers and accessories

SL HARDWOODS
390, Sydenham Road, Croydon
CRO 2EA, UK
Tel: 0845 004 8912
www.slhardwoods.co.uk
Extensive range of timbers, sheet materials, tools,
books and videos

CRAFT SUPPLIES LTD
The Mill, Millers Dale, Buxton
SK17 8SN, UK
Tel: 0800 146 417
www.craft-supplies.co.uk
Extensive range of timbers, veneers, tools, turning
accessories, consumables, books, videos and
courses

CHESTNUT PRODUCTS
PO Box 536, Ipswich
IP4 5WN, UK
Tel: 01473 425 878
www.chestnutproducts.co.uk
Extensive range of wood finishes and ancillary
products

WHITNEY SAWMILL
Old Vicarage, Clifford
HR3 5RY, UK
Tel: 01497 831656
Specialist supplier of selected exotic and native
timber

ROLSTON TIMBER
Hopp Cottage, Worchester Road
Leigh Sinton, WR13 5EQ, UK
Tel: 01886 833612
Specialist supplier of selected exotic and native
timber

HAFELE UK LTD
Swift Valley Industrial Estate, Rugby
CV21 1RD, UK
Tel: 01788 542020
www.hafele.co.uk
Huge range of furniture and hardware fittings

SUPPLIERS USA

BOSCH
Robert Bosch Tool Corp, 1800, W. Central Road
Mount Prospect, IL 60056
Tel: 224-232-2000
www.boschusa.com
Power tools and accessories

CLARKE POWER TOOLS INC.
28740 Glenwood Road, Perrysburg
Ohio 43551, USA
Tel: 800-227-9603
www.clarkeusa.com
Major supplier and manufacturer of woodworking
hand and power tools

CMT USA INC.
307-F Pomona Drive
Greensboro NC 27407, USA
Tel: 336-854-0201
www.cmtusa.com
Router bits and accessories

DEWALT (CUSTOMER SERVICE)
626 Hanover Pike
Hampstead MD 21074, USA
Tel: 1-800-433-9258
www.dewalt.com
Wide range of high-performance industrial
portable electric power tools and accessories

HITACHI POWER TOOLS
3950 Steve Reynolds Blvd
Norcross GA 30093, USA
Tel: 800-829-4752
www.hitachi.com
Compressors, generators and industrial machinery

JESADA TOOLS
310 Mears Boulevard
Oldsmar FL 34677 3047, USA
Tel: 813-891-6160
www. jesada.com
Router bits and accessories

MAKITA USA INC.
14930 Northam Street
La Mirada CA 90638, USA
Tel: 714-522-8088
www.makita.com
Power tools

METABO USA
Metabo Corporation
PO Box 2287, 1231 Wilson Drive
West Chester PA 19380, USA
Tel: 800-638-2264 `
www.metabousa.com
Power tools

TREND ROUTING TECHNOLOGY INC.
603 Memory Lane, Elizabethtown,
KY 42701, USA
Tel: 270-872-4674
www.trend-usa.com
Routers and accessories

HAFELE AMERICA
3901 Cheyenne Drive, PO Box 4000,
Archdale NC 27263, USA
Tel: 800-423-3531
www.hafele.com

FURTHER INFORMATION

Charlesworth, *David, David Charlesworth's Furniture-making Techniques* (Lewes: GMC Publications, 1999)

Charlesworth, *David, David Charlesworth's Furniture-making Techniques*
– Volume 2 (Lewes: GMC Publications, 2001)

Joyce, Ernest, *The Technique of Furniture Making, Fourth Edition* (London: Batsford, 1987; revised by Alan Peters)

Ley, Kevin, *Furniture Projects: Practical Designs for Modern Living* (Lewes: GMC Publications, 2000)

Ley, Kevin, *Furniture Projects with the Router* (Lewes: GMC Publications, 2002)

Ley, Kevin, *Furniture Workshop: A Woodworker's Guide* (Lewes: GMC Publications, 2004)

Moser, Thomas, *How to Build Shaker Furniture, Revised Edition* (New York: Sterling, 1980)

Peters, Alan, *Cabinetmaking – The Professional Approach* (London: Stobart, 1984)

www.photobox.co.uk/kevinley@btopenworld.com
Kevin Ley's photography album website, featuring images
of his furniture pieces.

www.linemine.com
Furniture plans are available to purchase online from
Furniture & Cabinet Making magazine's illustrator, Simon Rodway.

CONVERSION TABLE
inches to millimetres

in	mm	in	mm	in	mm	in	mm
1/64	0.3969	5/8	15.8750	2 3/4	69.8501	33	838.202
1/32	0.7937			2 7/8	73.0251	34	863.602
3/64	1.1906	41/64	16.2719	3	76.2002	35	889.002
1/16	1.5875	21/32	16.6687			36 (3ft)	914.402
5/64	1.9844	43/64	17.0656	3 1/8	79.3752		
3/32	2.3812	11/16	17.4625	3 1/4	82.5502	37	939.802
7/64	2.7781	45/64	17.8594	3 3/8	85.7252	38	965.202
1/8	3.1750	23/32	18.2562	3 1/2	88.9002	39	990.602
		47/64	18.6531	3 5/8	92.0752	40	1016.00
9/64	3.5719	3/4	19.0500	3 3/4	95.2502	41	1041.40
5/32	3.9687			3 7/8	98.4252	42	1066.80
11/64	4.3656	49/64	19.4469	4	101.500	43	1092.20
3/16	4.7625	25/32	19.8437			44	1117.60
13/64	5.1594	51/64	20.2406	5	127.000	45	1143.00
7/32	5.5562	13/16	20.6375	6	152.400	46	1158.40
15/64	5.9531	53/64	21.0344	7	177.800	47	1193.80
1/4	6.3500	27/32	21.4312	8	203.200	48 (4ft)	1219.20
		55/64	21.8281	9	228.600		
17/64	6.7469	7/8	22.2250	10	254.001	49	1244.60
9/32	7.1437			11	279.401	50	1270.00
19/64	7.5406	57/64	22.6219	12 (1ft)	304.801	51	1295.40
5/16	7.9375	29/32	23.0187			52	1320.80
21/64	8.3344	59/64	23.4156	13	330.201	53	1346.20
11/32	8.7312	15/16	23.8125	14	355.601	54	1371.60
23/64	9.1281	61/64	24.2094	15	381.001	55	1397.00
3/8	9.5250	31/32	24.6062	16	406.401	56	1422.20
		63/64	25.0031	17	431.801	57	1447.80
25/64	9.9219	1	25.4001	18	457.201	58	1473.20
13/32	10.3187			19	482.601	59	1498.60
27/64	10.7156	1 1/8	28.5751	20	508.001	60 (5ft)	1524.00
7/16	11.1125	1 1/4	31.7501	21	533.401		
29/64	11.5094	1 3/8	34.9251	22	558.801	61	1549.40
15/32	11.9062	1 1/2	38.1001	23	584.201	62	1574.80
31/64	12.3031	1 5/8	41.2751	24 (2ft)	609.601	63	1600.20
1/2	12.7000	1 3/4	44.4501			64	1625.60
		1 7/8	47.6251	25	635.001	65	1651.00
33/64	13.0969	2	50.8001	26	660.401	66	1676.40
17/32	13.4937			27	685.801	67	1701.80
35/64	13.8906	2 1/8	53.9751	28	711.201	68	1727.20
9/16	14.2875	2 1/4	57.1501	29	736.601	69	1752.60
37/64	14.6844	2 3/8	60.3251	30	762.002	70	1778.00
19/32	15.0812	2 1/2	63.5001	31	787.402	71	1803.40
39/64	15.4781	2 5/8	66.6751	32	812.802	72 (6ft)	1828.80

ABOUT THE AUTHOR

Kevin Ley retired from the Royal Air Force in 1987 and developed his hobby of furniture making into a successful business, designing and making bespoke pieces. He has been writing for GMC Publications for several years and now lives with his artist and teacher wife Yvonne in their picturesque cottage in a wooded nature reserve.

Kevin divides his time between making furniture in his workshop next to the house, writing and photography for the GMC woodworking magazines, working with Yvonne on the improvements to their cottage, and maintenance of their large garden. Both enjoy fast cars, reading, talking, music, sampling the delights of the local eating and watering holes, keeping fit and being in charge.

ACKNOWLEDGMENTS

My thanks to all the staff at GMC for their help with producing this book. Special thanks to Gerrie Purcell for commissioning the book, Virginia Brehaut and Gill Parris for the editing and Jo Patterson for such a great job on the design. Colin Eden-Eadon for his help and advice in publishing the original articles, Simon Rodway for his superb illustrations and plans, which show the construction so clearly and accurately, and of course to Jill and Jan for their cheerful greetings on the phone. They are all a real pleasure to work with.

My greatest thanks though are to my wife Yvonne for her encouragement and helpful criticism, contributions to furniture designs, proofreading, assistance with the photography, and patience with me and my sawdust!

INDEX

Contact us for a complete catalogue, or visit our website.
GMC Publications Ltd, 166 High Street, Lewes, East Sussex BN7 1XU, United Kingdom
Tel: 01273 488005 Fax: 01273 402866
www.gmcbooks.com